JAMAICAN
BAREFOOT BOY TO
MULTI-MILLIONAIRE

ALTIMAN G. DAVIS

TABLE OF CONTENTS

ACKNOWLEDGEMENTS

First and foremost, my deepest thanks go to my wife, Avril Davis, whose love, patience, and support have been the cornerstone of my life. Avril and I have shared a life full of adventure, sacrifice, and joy, and it is her partnership that has made so much of this story possible.

To my parents, Martha Evering and Norris Evering, I owe everything. Their hard work, strength, and wisdom laid the foundation upon which I built my life. Their sacrifices gave me the opportunities to strive for more, and their values continue to guide me each day.

A special thank you to my schoolteacher, Dr. Winston Marsh, who played a pivotal role in shaping my academic path and instilling in me a sense of purpose and discipline. His influence extended far beyond the classroom and helped mould the man I would become.

To all the friends, family, and mentors who have touched my life in ways both great and small – thank you. This book is not only my story, but a testament to the people who walked alongside me.

I would like to express my heartfelt thanks to those who have supported me throughout this journey.

PREFACE

This book will take you on a heartfelt journey through the life of a boy, Altiman (Alti) Davis, who grew up in the rural area of Jamaica. Born in poverty to a single mother in a one-room house, I never wore shoes to school until I was 14 years old. I faced countless challenges, including the ever-present temptation to follow the wrong path. Yet, despite the scarcity of material wealth, my childhood was always filled with love, happiness, and a sense of belonging. Thanks to the discipline and unwavering support of my parents, Martha Evering and Norris Evering. Their strict discipline and guidance kept me grounded and on the right path.

The purpose of writing this book is not to boast about my material success or the wealth I have acquired, but rather to serve as a testament to the resilience of the human spirit and the boundless potential within us all. It is a reminder that where you start in life does not dictate where you can go. With hard work, determination, a bit of intuition, and a touch of industriousness, it is possible to overcome the most daunting circumstances and carve a path to success.

These values, perseverance, integrity, and a strong work ethic, were instilled in me at an early age by my mother, a loving and hardworking woman who, despite our limited resources, always believed in the potential for greatness in her children. She wanted us to succeed not only academically but in whatever endeavors we chose to pursue. Her unwavering belief in us was the foundation that propelled us forward.

CHAPTER 1

Humble Beginnings in Rural Jamaica

I was the firstborn child of my single mother, Marther Hoilet, and we lived in a humble one-room thatched house nestled in the heart of rural Jamaica. The house was simple and modest, and our living conditions were basic, with an outhouse located about ten meters away for our sanitation needs. My mother would cook our meals over an open fire pit, a daily task that required careful attention. Our water source was equally basic, an in-ground tank that collected rainwater for all our domestic needs, which we used sparingly.

Although our home was isolated, our closest neighbours were my Uncle Reggie and Aunty Daisy, affectionately known to us as "Mamma." Despite being so close, their homes were not just a few steps away. To visit them, I had to walk several meters along a rugged, rocky dirt track that wound its way through the thick bushes. This path, though challenging, was a familiar part of my life. Uncle Reggie and Aunty Daisy had a large family of children, spanning various ages. I loved spending time with my cousins, as they were some of my closest companions and play-mates during my early years.

My mother, Martha Hoilet, was the youngest of fourteen children. Tragically, she had a twin sister who passed away as a baby. At just fourteen years old, my mother experienced another heartbreaking loss when her beloved mother died from a stroke at the age of 57. Despite these hardships, my mother grew up with a resilient spirit. She was quite the tomboy, known for her adven-turous nature. I fondly remember her climbing breadfruit, coco-nut, and ackee trees with ease.

Breadfruit, a large tree-borne fruit, was a staple of Jamaican cuisine. It has a round or oval shape and green, semi-smooth skin. When not quite mature, it is starchy and considered a vegetable, and as it matures, it turns a yellowish-brown colour. There are many ways to prepare it, but two of the most common methods are boiling it when it's still green or roasting it over an open fire when it begins to turn yellowish-brown. A delightful meal often involves roasted breadfruit served with butter and saltfish/cod-fish, but the ultimate Jamaican dish is breadfruit paired with ackee and saltfish, which is considered the national dish of Jamaica.

Ackee is a fruit that grows on a large tree. It starts in a green pod and, as it ripens, the pod transforms into a reddish-yellow colour. Once fully ripe, the pod bursts open to reveal a black seed and yellowish fruit. The seed is discarded, and the fruit is boiled and then mixed with saltfish and other ingredients to create a fla-vorful dish. Ackee was introduced to Jamaica from West Africa in the 18th century, and its name is derived from the West African term "Akye fufo." Saltfish, on the other hand, originates from Nova Scotia, Canada. It was traded to the West Indies in the 17th century in exchange for sugar and molasses. Saltfish became a common ingredient in Jamaican cuisine, particularly during the weekdays.

Sunday dinners were a special treat for my family. After weeks of fattening, the rooster we had been raising for months would finally make it to the dinner table. To prepare the rooster, it would be placed under an open basket with only its head sticking out. A swift chop with a machete would sever the head, and the chicken would run around for a few moments without its head. This, I think, was how the phrase "running around like a chicken without a head" came about. On rare occasions, when my mother could afford it, she would buy beef or goat from the local butcher, who sold his goods from the back of a donkey. Some days, a pickup truck would drive through the district, offering fresh fish for sale. These simple but meaningful experiences shaped my mother's life and our family's traditions, creating lasting memories of warmth and the unique flavors of Jamaica.

Our diet primarily consisted of rice and other starchy foods that we grew ourselves, including green bananas, yams, cassava, cocoa, sweet potatoes, and breadfruit. In addition, we cultivated a variety of vegetables, such as beans, peas, carrots, tomatoes, lettuce, and corn.

My mother is the family's historian, and she often shared with me the story of how our humble one-room thatched house came to be. According to her, this house was built by my grandfather, whom we affectionately called Daddy, for my grandmother Luna and my mother, as she was the youngest and still needed their support. After the passing of my grandmother, Luna, at 57 years old, Daddy and my mother remained in the house.

Before the one-room thatched house was built, there had been a larger two-room thatched house where Daddy, Luna, my mother, several older children, and some grandchildren lived, ten people in total. It became overcrowded, and Daddy realized the situation had become unsustainable. So, he decided to build the smaller one-bedroom thatched house nearby, which gave the older siblings a bit more living space, making their lives a bit more comfortable.

As my mother's older siblings reached adulthood, got married, and became financially independent, Daddy no longer needed to support them, which reduced his financial burden. He owned several pieces of land with coconut trees, and he worked on the land, earning a modest but steady income. With fewer responsibilities, Daddy was able to build a much larger home with a wood-shingled roof; it had two bedrooms, a living room, and a veranda.

For many years, this house served as the central gathering place for our family, hosting numerous family reunions, celebrations, and even weddings. It became the heart of our family's traditions and memories.

My mother was only eighteen years old when she became pregnant with me. To ensure a stable environment, my grandfather (Daddy) arranged for her to return to the modest one-room thatched house they had previously shared. It was in this small home that I was born on November 20, 1953, with the help of a local midwife.

At that time, most babies were born at home, as self-taught midwives attended deliveries. In our community, it was widely believed by children that airplanes were responsible for bringing babies to their parents. So, whenever a plane flew overhead, we children would shout at it, asking it to bring us a little baby. How innocent and naïve we were, not yet understanding the real process of childbirth.

CHAPTER 2

A Childhood of Simplicity and Survival

The year I was born, the population of Jamaica stood at 1,495,937, but by the time I was writing this book, the population had doubled, reaching close to 3 million.

Jamaica was still under British rule when I was a child. We used the British currency. Pound, shilling, and pence, and pledged our allegiance to Queen Elizabeth II, singing the British national anthem, "God Save the Queen."

Christmas was the happiest time of the year for me. I eagerly anticipated Santa Claus's arrival, believing that he would come through the window early on Christmas morning, bringing gifts while I was still asleep.

In preparation for the holiday, people painted their houses, as well as the stones surrounding flower gardens and sometimes the bases of trees in the yard, usually coconut trees. The festive season also meant the best meals of the year: curried goat, chicken, Christmas cakes, sweet potato pudding and sorrel wine. As I was raised in the Seventh-day Adventist faith, pork was never part of our diet, and many Jamaicans shared this practice.

On Christmas Day, we visited relatives, often enjoying two or three large dinners. Reflecting on those times, I realize that while I didn't receive many gifts, perhaps a few balloons, fire-crackers, a harmonica, a toy car, or a toy gun, I was among the happiest children.

On Christmas morning, tradition was to get together at dawn with my cousins and set off firecrackers. I was fortunate to grow up with a close-knit group of cousins, including Ray Llewellyn, Glasford Lindo (Nathan), Robin Hoilet, and many others. We spent much of our time together playing cricket, bird hunting, building our own scooters, and engaging in countless other activities. One of our favorite pastimes was finding the nests of the largest birds in Jamaica, the Bald Plate. These nests were often high up in tall trees, but we always managed to find a way to climb them and get the baby birds. We kept them in cages as pets, feeling proud of our little feathered companions.

Growing up, my mother had no choice but to cook all of our meals on an outdoor fire pit, as she was on her own and lacked the resources to build a proper outdoor kitchen like the one my Uncle Reggie and Aunt Daisy had. This method of cooking was quite common in rural Jamaica at that time, especially for families who didn't have modern amenities.

Our home was in a small district called Upton, nestled in the northeastern part of St. Ann, Jamaica. In Upton, nearly everyone had their own mini farms where they grew vegetables, raised free-range chickens, and kept goats, pigs, and sometimes even a cow. The pace of life was slow, and there wasn't much to do besides tending to the land, which left plenty of time for people to gossip about each other's business.

Respect for elders was deeply ingrained in our culture. It was considered unthinkable to pass an elder on the road without greeting them with a respectful "Good morning" or "Good evening." If you happened to walk by without offering a greeting, the elders would not hesitate to report your disrespect, and your parents would make sure you were corrected. This sense of respect was part of the fabric of daily life in Upton, shaping how the community interacted and maintained its values.

Upton was divided into two distinct areas: the poorer section to the west, where I was born, and the more affluent eastern section, which was home to wealthy expatriates from Britain, America, and Europe. The eastern part of Upton was a world apart from where I grew up. It was marked by large estates and sprawling properties, owned by influential foreigners who had come to Jamaica for both work and leisure. Among the notable features of this area were a cattle farm and the Upton Country Club, an 18-hole golf course that was the only one of its kind in the popular tourist town of Ocho Rios. The golf course served as a key attraction, catering to the influx of tourists who flocked to the area, and it still draws visitors today.

The expatriates lived in grand homes, many of which had been passed down through generations. These luxurious properties also provided employment for residents from surrounding districts. People worked as caddies on the golf course or maintained the lush grounds. Others worked as gardeners, chauffeurs, and housekeepers in the expatriates' sprawling estates. Some of the grand homes also served as guesthouses, welcoming European visitors to Jamaica.

Over the years, the expatriates began to leave, and the once-foreign properties were gradually taken over by affluent Jamaicans, marking a shift in the community. The landscape of Upton changed as it became a place where the wealth of the past merged with the growing prosperity of the future. The remnants of that earlier period, its mansions and golf courses, now stand as reminders of a time when foreign influence shaped the area.

CHAPTER 3

Family, Firepits, and First Lessons

I must have been around two or three years old when I first realized that it wasn't just my mother and I living in the house anymore. My stepfather, Uncle Norris, had started appearing more frequently. I can't pinpoint exactly when his visits began, but at some point, it became clear that he was now a permanent presence in our lives. His arrival marked a shift in the household dynamics that even my young mind could sense.

Before he came into the picture, I used to sleep with my mother in her bed. A warm and comforting arrangement. However, once he began staying with us, things changed. A small bed was made for me on the floor, signaling that I now had my own space, even if it felt like I was being gently pushed aside to make room for the new reality.

It was around this same age that I became aware of my younger brother, Valin. He was about two years younger than I was, though my memories of us together as babies are few and brief. One vivid memory, however, has stuck with me, a moment that could have ended in tragedy but fortunately didn't.

It was a rainy day, the kind where the world outside feels damp and alive. A pit had been dug in preparation for an outdoor toilet, and the rain had turned it into a water-filled hazard. Valin and I were playing near it, splashing in the puddles and mud, oblivious to any danger. At some point, he accidentally fell into the pit.

In my innocence, I wasn't alarmed. I thought Valin must have been a good swimmer because he appeared to be floating on the surface. I didn't see the urgency to alert my stepfather, who was babysitting us but was mostly inside the house, occasionally glancing out to check on us.

Then, in a flash, he must have noticed something was wrong. Bursting out of the house with the force of a charging tiger, he raced to the pit. Without hesitation, he grabbed Valin by his feet and hauled him out of the water. The moment was chaotic and terrifying, but also a testament to my stepfather's watchful eye and quick reflexes. That day could have ended very differently, and even as a child, I understood how close we had come to losing Valin.

Caring for two young boys who were close in age became overwhelming for my mother, so my brother Valin was sent to live with my stepfather's mother, affectionately called "Mammy," in another district. This arrangement was not unusual in Jamaica during that time. For single mothers facing challenges in raising multiple children, it was common for one or more to be sent to live with other family members who could help shoulder the responsibility.

From this point on, any reference I make to "my father" refers to Uncle Norris, who played a consistent and supportive role throughout my life. My biological father, on the other hand, was absent, and I had no relationship with him.

At the age of five, I began attending Basic School, which is the equivalent of kindergarten. In rural Jamaica at the time, Basic School teachers did not require formal training. Anyone with basic literacy, a grasp of civic knowledge, and some understanding of arithmetic could establish and run a Basic School. However, there were teachers with more advanced education who had completed high school or passed proficiency exams, such as the 1st Year, 2nd Year, or 3rd Year exams, which were precursors to the Jamaica School Certificate (JSC) and O-Levels. O-Levels, administered by the University of Cambridge and London, were rigorous examinations taken at the end of high school and served as prerequisites for higher education. These exams were widely recognized across Jamaica and other Commonwealth countries.

After completing Basic School, my mother enrolled me in a private school run by the Seventh-day Adventist Church. Unlike public schools, this institution did not receive government funding. Among my cousins, I was the only one attending this private school, as they were enrolled in a government-funded public school in a different district. At the time, my mother was not affiliated with any religion, so I believe her decision to send me to the Seventh-day Adventist school was influenced by my father. He had grown up attending the church alongside his parents and likely saw value in its teachings and education system.

When I was about nine years old, my mother was still cooking on an outdoor fire pit, which presented significant challenges, especially during the rainy season. Watching her struggle to prepare meals in those conditions inspired me to act. Determined to

11

make her life easier, I decided to build a kitchen that would provide her with shelter from the rain. Even at that young age, I had a knack for using my hands to solve problems.

Living in the bush, we were surrounded by an abundance of trees, so I set to work selecting manageable ones to cut down for my project. Coconut trees were also plentiful in the area, and I gathered branches from them to use as roofing material. To construct an elevated fire pit, I collected an assortment of small rocks. With these materials in hand, I spent several weeks painstakingly building an enclosed kitchen. The walls were made from the trees I had cut, while the roof was crafted from the coconut tree branches. For the fire pit, I carefully arranged the rocks to ensure they were both sturdy and functional. When I finally completed the structure, my mother's joy and gratitude made all the effort worthwhile.

Life in our rural district was not without its challenges, but as children, we accepted them as part of our everyday existence. For instance, to get to school, I had to walk about five miles each way on a dirt road, always barefoot. The path was littered with rocks, and roots from nearby trees sometimes sprawled across it, waiting to trip you up if you were inattentive. Yet, we didn't dwell on the difficulties we had to endure. Over time, our little feet grew so tough that cuts and bruises often went unnoticed until we stepped into the aluminum tubs used for washing ourselves before bed.

Despite the distance, the daily trek to my Basic School didn't feel like a burden. In fact, it became a joyful adventure. My friends and I would run along the path, laughing and playing as we flew kites made from whatever materials we could find. Some kites were fashioned from broad leaves plucked from chocolate trees, with simple threads tied to make them soar. Others were made from scraps of paper taken from our writing books, reinforced with coconut tree straws to give them structure. Those moments, filled with laughter and ingenuity, remain some of the fondest memories of my childhood.

Growing up in a small, one-room thatched house, I was surrounded by cousins of various age groups. Our home was filled with laughter and creativity, but not with material wealth. Store-bought toys were a rare luxury, only gifted to us during Christmas when Santa brought them. This made those moments feel magical, but for the rest of the year, we relied on our resourcefulness to create our own entertainment.

CHAPTER 4

Cousins, Creativity, and Country Life

Birthdays were not events we eagerly anticipated. Looking back, I now realize that financial constraints likely made it difficult for our families to plan parties or special celebrations. My birthday would come and go unnoticed, often passing without so much as a mention. Days or weeks later, I would realize it had already passed. This wasn't just my experience but a common reality for the children I grew up with, however, this has changed since adulthood and even more so when the children came into our lives.

In the absence of toys, we turned to our imaginations and the natural materials around us. One of our favorite pastimes was making toy cars. We would cut a section of a banana tree trunk, carefully fashioning it into the car's body. Using sticks as axles, we attached unripe oranges to the ends to serve as wheels. A simple string tied to the car allowed us to pull it along, and we would spend hours parading our creations around. As we grew older and our skills improved, we graduated to making toy cars from wood, adding details and sturdier construction.

Another game involved old, worn-out car tires. We would place sturdy sticks inside the tires and push them along as we ran behind, laughing and shouting as the tires rolled ahead. This simple activity often turned into spirited races, each of us determined to prove who was the fastest.

These moments, though simple and born out of necessity, taught us creativity, camaraderie, and resilience. They are some of my most cherished memories, a testament to the joy that can be found in life's simplest pleasures.

Children in Jamaica are always running, whether on our way to school or while playing on the playground. We often invented our own games or modified ones that we inherited from our parents. One such game was called "Chebby-Chase." Although the exact origin of the game is unclear, I suspect it may have roots in the hardships faced by our ancestors, particularly the enslaved people who, during their brutal conditions, had to devise such activities to keep their spirits up and temporarily escape the suffering imposed upon them by their oppressive masters.

The game itself was simple yet exciting. Two lines were drawn on the ground at opposite ends of an open area, usually 50 to 100 feet apart. Each team would station its players at their respective lines, which were referred to as the "Base." The objective was for one team to chase a member of the opposing team. If the chaser caught the runner before they returned to their Base, the runner would be eliminated from the game.

Here's how the game worked: For simplicity, let's refer to the teams as Team A and Team B. A coin toss or other random method would determine which team would be the first to send a player out from their Base to initiate the chase. Suppose Team-A lost the draw. A player from Team-A would then leave the Base, trying to lure a runner from Team-B to chase after them. The runner from Team B would begin pursuing the Team-A player, but to help protect the runner, Team A would send another player to chase down the Team-B runner. The goal for each player was to return safely to their Base without being caught. If a player was caught, they would be eliminated. The team that ended up with an empty base, the team whose players were all eliminated, would lose the game.

This game could go on for an extended period, as there was no set limit to the distance players could travel. It may sound a bit complicated, but it was a highly popular game, and we had an incredible amount of fun playing it.

In a way, you could think of the game as analogous to a World War II scenario, where a B-17 bomber would fly over Germany to unload its bombs and then return to base without being shot down. While en route, a German Messerschmitt BF 109 might catch wind of the bomber and initiate a chase. The information about the chase would be relayed to the RAF, who would then deploy a Spitfire or Mustang fighter to intercept the Messerschmitt, engaging in a dogfight so that the bomber could complete its mission and return to base safely. Much like the game of "Chebby-Chase," the bomber or the runner had to be strategic and resourceful to make it back to safety.

One of our favorite pastimes was venturing into the woods to hunt birds, using various methods like our trusty slingshots, setting up a "Gum Pole," constructing a "Calabash," or utilizing a "Spring." Each technique was a surefire way to ensure we returned home with a bounty of birds for a feast. Let me briefly explain how each method worked.

16

The "Gum Pole" was crafted from a small branch, typically stripped of its leaves, with two or three smaller branches jutting out from it. To create the sticky substance that would attract the birds, we would extract sap from a breadfruit tree and combine it with brown sugar, boiling it down into a thick, tacky paste. This paste was then carefully applied to the smaller branches. Once prepared, we would climb a tree and hoist the Gum-Pole high into the branches, waiting quietly, hidden from the birds' sight. As soon as the birds landed on the sticky branches, we would swiftly pull the pole down and capture the unlucky bird.

The "Calabash" was a trap made by bounding small, leafless tree branches together to form a dome, usually around one foot by one foot in size, depending on the type of birds we were targeting. Beneath the dome, we would place orange seeds or other berries that the birds found irresistible. A stick would prop up one side of the Calabash, creating a small opening where the birds could access the food. Once the birds pecked at the seeds, they would inadvertently disturb the stick, causing the Calabash to fall and trap them inside. Sometimes, we would soak the seeds in overproof white rum we had secretly swiped from our parents' stock, which would intoxicate the birds, making them easier to catch.

The "Spring" trap involved using a flexible branch anchored at one end to the ground and bent into an arch at the other. At the top of the arch, a looped string was tied, with three sticks placed under it to maintain the tension on the branch. We would scatter bird seeds within the looped area. When a bird entered the loop to eat the seeds, it would disturb the string, releasing the tension and causing the loop to tighten, trapping the bird.

Each of these methods required patience and precision, but when successful, they always guaranteed us a feast of fresh birds as we plucked their feathers, gutted them, and roasted them over an open fire.

My cousins and I always looked forward to visiting our grandfather (Daddy), as he had a special way of making us feel free and cherished. He would give us his finest fruits and, in his own way, offer us complete freedom to enjoy ourselves however we liked. One of my most memorable moments was when, after I had carefully cut up his tobacco into small pieces for his pipe, he let me take a puff. It was a rare and exciting experience that made me feel all grown-up.

His name was Robert Hoilett, though we all lovingly called him Daddy. He was the patriarch of a large family, with twelve children, each of whom had several children of their own. This made for lively, bustling gatherings at his house whenever all the cousins came together.

Daddy was a tall, handsome man who carried himself with a quiet elegance and grace. He walked with dignity, and the way he smoked his pipe left a trail of smoke that billowed like a steam train in motion. We all adored him, and there was something magical about being in his presence, soaking up the wisdom and warmth he shared so freely.

He often told us stories about his childhood and the generations that came before him. His grandparents had been born into slavery, but they gained their freedom in 1838 when slavery was abolished in Jamaica. This made me just four generations removed from that painful history, a fact that always struck me deeply. I would listen intently to his stories, absorbing every word like a sponge.

One of my favorite stories was the song he would sing to us: "1, 2, 3, Colo Man a come, asked him the time, him look upon the sun." This song had its roots in the building of the Panama Canal in the early 1900s, during which many Jamaicans migrated to Panama for work. They lived in a place called Colon, which still has a large Jamaican community to this day, keeping their culture alive. These workers made good money, enabling them to buy luxury items such as watches. However, when they returned to Jamaica and walked through the streets showing off their new watches, if someone asked them the time, they couldn't read the watches. Instead, they would look up at the sun, using the position of their shadows to estimate the time, as they had done before the advent of modern watches. This humorous yet touching tale was one of many that brought our family's history to life in a way that still resonates with me today.

CHAPTER 5

<hr />

The Big Move

In 1963, the year after Jamaica gained independence, my family and I made a significant move. I was around ten years old at the time, and we relocated to a larger house where my father, Norris, my grandmother, Mammy, and my brother, Valin, had been living. I don't remember much about the logistics of the move, as there wasn't much to transport from our small one-room thatched house. However, I do recall that it was just my mother, my sister Sherron, my newborn brother Leslie, and I. My youngest sister, Colleen, wasn't born yet.

The excitement of this new chapter was noticeable. Our new house was right next to a playground, which meant there were always children to play with. Saturdays were especially lively, as a cricket match would take place every weekend, attracting the entire community to watch. Moving to this bigger district was a life-changing experience for me, as it was the first time I had ever lived in an area with electricity. In our old district of Upton, there was no electricity. We relied on glass kerosene lamps with "Home Sweet Home" written on their shades. For additional light, we used homemade lamps made from bottles filled with kerosene oil, with a wick sticking out to be lit with a match. We also created makeshift torches by binding coconut tree branches, which gave off an intense, bright light and a lot of heat.

Our new home was perched on top of a hill, right by the main road that ran through the district. The house had a gate with two columns, each topped with two statues of lions. My grandfather, Leopold Evering, had earned a reputation in the district for his sense of status and influence. In the 1950s, this new house was one of the largest in the area, complete with a veranda and two small bedrooms on the left side of the veranda. The living room was located directly behind the veranda, with large, textured, frosted glass doors running along its entire length, offering a sense of openness. Behind the living room was the dining room, and beyond that, the pantry, which was nearly as small as the dining area itself. At the back of the pantry was the kitchen, which featured a wood-burning elevated firepit. Above the firepit was a chimney that extended through the roof, venting smoke from the firewood used to cook our meals.

The roof of the house was made of heavy gray Mexican tiles that had weathered countless hurricanes over the years. However, despite these features, the house lacked indoor plumbing or running water. Our toilet was a small outdoor structure located several feet away from the house, which was typical for most people in the district. Our primary source of water came from rainwater, which was collected in a steel drum placed at the side of the house. There was also a community standpipe located centrally within the district where everyone could collect fresh water. We were fortunate enough to own a donkey, which helped transport two large containers of water from the standpipe, saving us from carrying the water on our heads like many others in the district had to do.

We took our baths behind the house in an aluminum tub, in an open space partially covered by sheets of zinc. Bathing twice a day was the norm, once in the morning before school and again in the evening before bed. Some evenings, though, we would stop at the river on our way home from school to take a refreshing dip. It wasn't entirely private in our backyard, as some neighbours used it as a shortcut, so I built a makeshift bathroom with sticks and large crocus bags to give us a bit of privacy.

After my grandfather's (Leopold Evering) death, the responsibility of managing the business fell to my grandmother (Mammy) and her children, my father Norris and aunt Joyce. My father took over the responsibilities as Joyce was married and living elsewhere. Looking back, I don't think my father was the most effective businessman. The ventures that my grandfather had left behind began to deteriorate over time. I remember the shop in front of our house, which had been rented out to a man named Mr. Jacob Hay from a nearby district. The shop included living quarters and a grocery store, but once the tenant moved out, the building fell into disrepair and eventually had to be torn down.

This new chapter in our lives brought with it new experiences, opportunities, and challenges, marking a significant shift in how we lived, worked, and interacted with the world around us.

CHAPTER 6

The Two Who Raised Me

My mother is an incredible woman, one whose strength and talent continue to inspire me. She worked tirelessly in the fields, planting a wide variety of crops. Bananas, yams, sweet potatoes, beans, peas, tomatoes, corn, cassava, and many others. Her work ethic was unmatched, and she took great pride in providing for our family.

In addition to her farming skills, my mother was also an exceptionally gifted seamstress. She could create beautiful dresses without ever needing a pattern. All her creations were worn with pride, including the school uniforms for my sisters and I, and she even made me a swimming trunk once. Her talent was a testament to her creativity and resourcefulness.

Above all, my mother's greatest priority was our happiness and safety. She had me when she was just 18 years old, but surprisingly, neither my brother Valin nor I ever referred to her as "Mom." Instead, we always called her Aunt Tit, a name given to her by her father, whom we called Daddy. It wasn't that we didn't love her deeply, but perhaps because she was so young when she had us, she preferred that we not address her as a typical "Mom." In Jamaican culture, it's common for people to have pet names, and my pet name was Pero, also given to me by Daddy.

She was a warm, loving, and generous person who would do anything for others. Our home felt like an open door to anyone in need. Over the years, I've witnessed more than a dozen children come and go. Some of whom were relatives who had disagreement with their parents, others whose parents had moved abroad, and some whose parents worked in live-in jobs at guesthouses and couldn't take their children with them. Our home was a safe haven for them all, a place where they could find refuge and comfort.

Later in life, whenever my mother visited Jamaica, she threw a huge party that everyone in the district attended. It's a testament to the lasting love and respect people have for her. But despite her nurturing and kind nature, she could also be tough when necessary. I remember one time when she sent me to gather firewood for our dinner. Instead of going to get the firewood, I went to the field to play cricket. When I returned at supper time, I found my meal waiting for me, but when I lifted the cover, I was shocked to find that all the food was raw! My mother had left it uncooked as a lesson for me, and that experience taught me to never again neglect my duties. From then on, I made sure the firewood was always ready when needed.

As I mentioned earlier, she was the ultimate tomboy and a true "badass" in every sense of the word. No one dared mess with her children. If you did, she was coming for you. Growing up as teenagers in the country, there wasn't much to do for entertainment unless you attended church on certain nights for sing-along meetings or went to the local rum bars, which were just as well-known and frequented as the churches. I was a devout churchgoer,

24

so I didn't hang out at the rum bars. Instead, I spent my evenings walking the dark streets with my friends, as there were no street-lights to guide our way, hoping to run into a few girls. Girls were a rare sight at night, as they weren't typically allowed out unless they sneaked away. The only light on those streets came from the glow of the churches during services, the houses near the roads, and the ever-constant illumination from the rum bars, which were open all night long.

One night, my friends and I decided to stand by the fence of a church, making fun of some of the congregation members who were "speaking in tongues," uttering what seemed like gibberish. I had grown up in a very quiet Seventh-day Adventist church, where we didn't even clap our hands during songs. We simply said "Amen" to everything, with no shouting of "Hallelujah" or "Praise the Lord."

As we stood there, laughing and poking fun, a big, burly man from the congregation came out and slapped me across the face. Instantly, I reacted, fighting back, and before I knew it, a full-blown brawl started. The word quickly reached my mother, and in an instant, she was there. The man who had slapped me was identified, and my mother, furious, lunged at him like a lioness protecting her cubs. She grabbed him by his testicles, squeezing and dragging him around like a rag doll as he screamed, "Let go of my balls!" It took a few people to pull my mother off him, but no one could deny that she was one fierce protector.

About my father, Norris Ivan Evering, he was a solid, tall man, standing at around six feet. By trade, he was a carpenter, but he was also skilled in various other trades. He dabbled in ma-sonry, horseshoeing, and road paving, excelling in each. One of his jobs in road paving involved handling a custom-made tar dis-penser. He would spread the hot tar from this handheld device while others followed behind, covering it with gravel. The job was grueling, and sometimes he would come home with painful burns from the hot tar on his hands.

I distinctly recall one summer holiday when my cousin Ray Llewlyn and I worked with him on a project. He had us mix the concrete for a water tank he was building. We were paid ten shillings a day, a generous sum for us at the time. Despite his many skills, my father was never the disciplinarian in our household. That role fell to my mother. Though he had a loud voice, his bark was worse than his bite, and we all knew it as children.

Norris was the son of Leopold Evering and Sarah Evering, and he had a sister named Joyce. Leopold, his father, was a highly influential man in the district and had a fair amount of wealth. He passed away in 1955, the same year my brother Valin was born. Unfortunately, I have no memory of what he looked like, as I believe he was in his 50s or 60s when he passed away.

Leopold and Sarah were active members of the Seventh-day Adventist Church and were regarded as one of the wealthiest couples in the community. Leopold owned several properties, the largest being a 20-acre plot with numerous pimento and lime trees, which were regularly harvested and sold in the market. He also had dairy cows, owned a grocery store with a residence attached, and carried a pistol. A symbol of status in those days.

My father was ten years older than my mother, and though my biological father had no role in my upbringing, I've always wondered why my last name wasn't changed to Evering. Norris, after all, was the father figure who raised me during my childhood.

Growing up, I had no relationship with my biological father until I turned 16. During that time in Jamaica, it was relatively common for some fathers to distance themselves from their children, likely to avoid paying child support or simply because they didn't want to form an attachment at such a young age. My relationship with my biological father only began when he was preparing to be ordained as a minister in his church and felt the need to come clean about his past.

I clearly remember that my father, Norris, was not happy about the idea of my biological father entering my life at that point. My biological father's name was Vincent Davis, and I share a striking resemblance to him. Growing up, Vincent had never acknowledged my existence. In fact, whenever our paths crossed, he would ignore me. It was my grandmother, Mammy, who persuaded my father, Norris, to reconsider his stance. She told him, "The boy is now 16 years old, and a little extra help would be good for him."

Eventually, my father, Norris, accepted that Vincent would now be a part of my life. Not long after that, Vincent asked me to visit the local store, Uncle Jim's, to try on a pair of Bata shoes. I remember they were black snakeskin shoes. I liked them, and he bought them for me. To this day, those shoes were the only thing I ever received from him before his passing.

Vincent's wife, Miss Edna, was a kind-hearted woman who genuinely wanted me to form a connection with my half-siblings, Donna and Dean, at the time. She encouraged me to spend time with them, so I would visit their home occasionally when they were out at church or otherwise. Over time, I forged a strong relationship with my half-siblings: Donna, Dean, Randal, Adene, Ann, and Garner.

Today, I have a meaningful bond with them, and I am grateful for the family connections that grew from an unlikely and late start.

CHAPTER 7

The Seventh-Day Adventist Church

After completing basic school and kindergarten at around five years old, I was enrolled in a private school run by the Seventh-day Adventist Church. By this time, my mother, Sherron, Leslie, and I had moved into my father's house with Mammy and Valin. Our new home was only about a five-minute walk from my school, a sharp contrast to the many miles I had previously walked barefoot to get to school five days a week.

Looking back, I didn't understand why my mother chose the Seventh-day Adventist School for me, especially since neither she nor my father were members of the church at that time. However, many years later, my mother was baptized, and my father was re-baptized. My father had once been a member of the church in his younger years, as it was the church his parents attended. Over time, however, he stopped going and enjoyed spending time at rum bars with his friends.

The Seventh-day Adventist School, being much closer to our new house, meant I no longer had to walk miles to school. The school itself was housed in an open church hall. During the week, it served as a school, and on Saturdays, it was converted back into a church. Inside, there were no physical barriers between the classes, just imaginary lines that separated them. I assumed I had been sent to this school because it was operated by the church that Mammy attended.

It seemed like there were no clear standards for how the school was run, as there was no structured curriculum. As a result, school attendance began to decline rapidly due to a lack of trained teachers. That was until a young, energetic teacher named Winston E. Preddie arrived. A graduate of the Seventh-day Adventist College (then known as West Indies College, now Northern Caribbean University), he took charge and quickly turned the school around.

Winston was a true savior of the school. His leadership brought rapid improvements, and he earned the love and admiration of everyone in the district. Parents whose children attended other schools noticed the changes and decided to register their kids at the Seventh-day Adventist School. He introduced a variety of extracurricular activities, including the church's Pathfinder Club, an arts and crafts club, cave exploration, and more.

Unfortunately, Winston's time at the school was short-lived, lasting only about two years, much to the devastation of the students and parents who adored him. Due to his success in revitalizing the school, the Seventh-day Adventist Conference Board, which operated the school, decided to transfer him to Port Maria Academic High School, a school that was struggling at the time. Port Maria Academy was located in the neighbouring parish of St. Mary.

The Seventh-day Adventist Church, a prominent denomination in Jamaica, was founded in the United States in 1863. One of its key co-founders was Ellen G. White, whose teachings and writings remain influential within the church to this day.

I would describe the Seventh-day Adventist Church as a blend of several religious practices. For example, its members observe the Sabbath, a day of rest and worship, which begins at sunset on Friday and ends at sunset on Saturday. Certain dietary restrictions are observed, such as the avoidance of pork, shellfish, and certain seafood like shrimp, crab, and fish without scales.

Additionally, there were strict guidelines for women, including prohibitions on wearing pants, straightening their hair, listening to secular music, consuming alcohol, attending dance parties, smoking, and engaging in premarital sex. Although my own beliefs have changed and I no longer follow these doctrines, I can speak to the rigid standards that defined the church during my time as a member.

Like many other Christian denominations, the Seventh-day Adventist Church teaches the belief in the Second Coming of Christ, and supports the fact that after death, people are either sent to heaven or hell based on their actions. The church also shares a common practice with other religions in that parts of the Bible are often interpreted to support personal beliefs, and when one sins, there is always the option of seeking forgiveness through prayer.

I remember an event from my childhood that highlights some of these beliefs. There was a man, whom we initially assumed was a Rastafarian because of the headwrap he wore. At the time, Rastafarians were looked down upon by many in the church, partly because their practices included smoking marijuana, which the church disapproved of. However, we later learned that this man was not a Rastafarian, but a Sikh, which was an unfamiliar religion in rural Jamaica at that time.

The incident started when the Sikh man, who had fallen in love with the daughter of one of our church members, allegedly drugged and held her captive, trying to persuade her to marry him. Fortunately, she managed to escape. On one Sabbath, as we were attending church, we were informed by a lookout that the Sikh man was returning to retrieve the woman. The lookout, mistakenly identifying him as a Rastafarian, warned the church that "Rasta man gaan a Gull," meaning the man was heading to the church member's home to take his daughter back.

As the whispers made it through out the congregation, the church service was abruptly interrupted, and all the men rushed home to arm themselves. Some grabbed machetes, and one even fetched a shotgun, and together we hurried to the house in the gully, located between two hills. As a young boy, the excitement of the situation pulled me in, and despite my mother's protests, I joined the group.

When we arrived, both sides of the gully were lined with men, holding machetes and rocks, ready to confront the Sikh man's car. It became clear that the poor man had no chance of escape, and the police had to intervene to rescue him from the angry crowd.

This event, while unsettling in retrospect, serves as a powerful memory of the intense and sometimes misguided passion that defined that period in my life as a Seventh-day Adventist.

Before marriage, sexual relations were strictly prohibited, but this didn't stop some of us young people from engaging in such activities. We rationalized it by thinking we could always seek forgiveness through prayer afterward. The friends I kept were mostly those who attended church, not just from my own congregation, but from others as well. As a result, I never mingled with people who indulged in smoking ganja or weed. I've never smoked cigarettes or ganja in my life, which many find hard to believe. Especially non-Jamaicans who often stereotype us, assuming all Jamaicans smoke weed.

Even though I no longer practice the religion, I continue to hold onto the moral values and principles I was taught. I still believe in some of the lessons I learned, and I often find myself whispering a quiet prayer to myself.

CHAPTER 8

Barefoot Days and River Ways

After Winston Preddie left our school, we got a new principal, but things started to go downhill. Eventually, my mother made the decision to transfer me to a government-run school. It was called Newstead All-Age School, located in the neighbouring parish of St. Mary, separated from us by the White River. At the time, I wasn't happy with the change. I had to leave most of my friends behind, and the new school was much farther from home, requiring me to walk a long way barefoot on a rugged dirt road filled with rocks and tree roots.

Many children from my district also walked barefoot to school, so it wasn't unusual. Still, the rough terrain often left me with cuts and bruises, and as I mentioned before, these were only discovered when I was getting ready for bed.

I had a pair of shoes, but they were only for church or special occasions like weddings, school trips, and funerals. Wearing them to school was out of the question. I also had a few homemade slippers that I made with wood and parts of old discarded leather shoes. I only wore it at home as they weren't durable enough for the school journey. They would have slowed me down, so I couldn't wear them to school. I made those wooden slippers by shaping bits of discarded wood and asking Mass But, the local shoemaker, for old shoes. He'd give me leather strips from shoes people had thrown away. I would cut the leather, shape the wood to fit my feet, and then nail the leather to the wood to create make-shift slippers.

Later in this book, you'll read about how I took this ingenuity to new heights.

We all wore school uniforms. The boys wore beige khaki pants, and the girls wore blue dresses. My uniform pants often had patches on them because they were torn or worn out from frequent use. It was hard for my mother to afford new ones, so she made sure to stretch their lifespan by patching them with similar fabrics.

I clearly remember the first time I got a pair of shoes for school. I was fourteen, and many of my friends had already been wearing shoes. Some of them had relatives abroad who sent money or older siblings who worked and helped at home, which was common in Jamaica. One day, a very affordable shoe all in one rubber shoe called Tarzan hit the market. They only came in black or brown, and that was my first pair of school shoes. They were all rubber, so my feet would get hot and sweaty, especially since I spent most of my time in the sun. But I didn't mind. Finally, I had school shoes.

I have recently visited my old school, Newstead Primary School in Jamaica, and I have noticed that there were still students walking to school without any shoes. I have reached out to the school and requested that they send me the number of students without shoes and their sizes. I will be making sure that these children will never have to walk barefoot to school anymore.

Looking back, as I stood there watching those barefoot children, I couldn't help but reflect on the sacrifices my own mother made to ensure I got an education despite the hardships we faced. It reminded me how much of my life was shaped by her decisions, big and small.

In our home, it was always my mother who made sure we stayed on the right path, even when resources were scarce. She was the force behind every step we took, from getting to school to staying focused on our goals. It's evident that my mother was the decision-maker in our family, as is common in many Jamaican households. Even though my father was present, all decisions concerning us children, from school trips to playing football or cricket with friends were made by my mother. We would never ask our father; it was always my mother.

To get to my new school, we had to cross the White River, which separated St. Ann and St. Mary. This river supplied two hydroelectric stations that provided power to much of Jamaica. The school was right by the river, which often tempted some of my friends to skip school and go fishing or swimming instead. Although I was sometimes tempted to join them, I knew that if my mother found out, I would face serious consequences, so I resisted.

Thanks to the creativity and resourcefulness of a few young men from my district, a once humble stretch of river has now become one of Jamaica's most natural and popular tourist attractions, known as the Blue Hole.

Years ago, this very spot was a gathering place for the mothers in our community, who would come together to wash their clothes. Washing day was an event everyone looked forward to. It was a lively, fun-filled time for both mothers and their children. It was also the place where much of the local gossip was exchanged, as the day would be spent scrubbing, chatting, and bonding. My mother's designated washing day was Monday, and I had a specific role to play. On my way to school, I would carry a large aluminum tub filled with dirty clothes and drop it off at the river. Then, after school, I would return to collect the freshly washed clothes, which would have been dried in the sun, and head back home.

However, during school holidays, things were different. The children would join their mothers at the river for the washing routine, and this was the only time the girls were allowed to visit the river. A privilege always granted to the boys. Washing day during the holidays felt more like a celebration; it was a joyous occasion, almost like a picnic. We would swim and play in the water all day and enjoy a delicious cookout, often consisting of roasted breadfruit, butter, and salt fish.

Growing up in rural Jamaica, there were no formal swimming lessons. Swimming was something we learned on our own, out of necessity and fun. However, because the girls had limited opportunities to go to the river, many never learned to swim. Hopefully, this has changed over the years, and girls today have more chances to enjoy and learn the joys of swimming in the river, just like the boys always did.

CHAPTER 9

The Education My Mother Fought For

Education was always a cornerstone of my upbringing, thanks to my mother's firm belief that education was the key to success in life. She made it clear that missing school was never an option unless we were seriously ill. Only then were we allowed to stay home. Education was non-negotiable. She also took an active interest in our progress, attending all parent-teacher meetings to stay informed about our academic performance.

We didn't have a television in our home, which meant there were no distractions from our studies. Instead, we focused on completing our homework and reading, ensuring that we stayed on top of our schoolwork.

I recall a notable program that was a lifeline for many students. An initiative funded by the United States, in collaboration with the Jamaican government, to provide hot lunches to schoolchildren. This program was a godsend, especially for families who struggled to provide nutritious meals. It supplied essential food products like flour, cornmeal, bulgur wheat, and other staples. At the start of each school year, trucks would deliver large bags of these food items to schools.

Parents would volunteer on a rotating schedule to prepare the meals, ensuring that every child received a hot lunch every school day. This initiative not only alleviated the burden on parents, who often found it challenging to provide meals for their children, but it also guaranteed that students had at least one healthy meal each day. It was a brilliant program that made a significant difference in the lives of many families.

Sadly, after decades of operation, the program was discontinued, leaving parents to find alternative ways to feed their children. For some, this meant their children missed school because their families couldn't afford the lunch money.

I vividly remember one week when my mother didn't have enough lunch money to send us to school. Instead of letting us stay home, she prepared a humble meal of green bananas and flour dumplings, drizzled with a bit of coconut oil. She would meet us by the river, away from the eyes of our classmates, so we wouldn't face ridicule. There was a stigma attached to being poor, and we knew we would be made fun of if others saw our modest meal. But despite the circumstances, we ate our lunch with contentment, and with spirits undampened, we returned to school. It was a moment that underscored not just the value of education but also the resilience and resourcefulness that often came out of necessity.

While my mother ensured we never missed a day of school, the experience went far beyond just attending classes. School was more than textbooks and lessons. It was where we learned about life, friendships, and the wider world beyond our small community. One of the most exciting parts of school life, for me, was the annual school trips. These trips opened my eyes to places I had only heard about and sparked a hunger to experience life beyond the hills of our district.

Every year, most schools in Jamaica organized exciting school trips, and for us, country kids, these trips were an event we eagerly anticipated for months in advance. The trips provided a chance to venture beyond our rural communities and explore the bustling city of Kingston, which was home to many of the country's prominent manufacturing companies. Our visits often included tours of various facilities such as the textile company, D&G, where popular sodas were made, a sugar plantation, and a cookie factory. But perhaps the most thrilling part of the trip was visiting Hope Gardens, which featured a zoo with exotic animals and an amusement park. These destinations were like a dream come true for us kids who had grown up far from the busy city life.

However, these trips came with a cost, and it was often difficult for my mother to find the money for them. I wanted to help ease the financial burden, so I came up with an idea to earn my own money. I asked my mother to help me make some inexpensive homemade desserts that I could sell at school. She made a dessert called Drops. Shredded coconut mixed with brown sugar and boiled to a thick paste, which solidified as it cooled. In addition to the Drops, I also made other desserts such as Gizzada and Pink Top. Gizzada was a small pastry filled with a sweet mixture of grated coconut and brown sugar, giving it a rich, brownish colour. Pink Top, on the other hand, was made by combining coconut with white sugar, with half of it coloured pink. When the two halves were joined, the result was a delightful dessert with a pink top and white bottom.

I would bring these homemade desserts to school and sell them for a lower price than Miss Phillipa, the regular vendor who sold the same items. By undercutting her prices, I managed to make enough money not only to cover the cost of my school trip but also to have plenty of pocket money left over. It was a great feeling knowing that I could contribute and make the most of this exciting opportunity.

CHAPTER 10

From Pimento Trees to Schoolhouse Dreams

My father controlled a few parcels of land, each spanning multiple acres, which had been inherited by Mammy following the death of her husband, Leopold. One of these properties was particularly valuable, as it contained a mix of livestock and fruit trees. Among the animals were cows and goats, and the land was dotted with a variety of pimento and lime trees, all of which were carefully cultivated for profit. The pimento trees, in particular, were an important source of income, and we often hired additional help to harvest them, as the task required significant effort, given the number of trees on the property.

Harvesting the pimento was a meticulous process. Using tree clippers, we would carefully cut the branches heavily laden with berries. The unripe, green berries were then hand-picked from the branches and placed in straw baskets, while the ripe, purple berries were discarded. Once the day's work was done, the baskets of green pimento were loaded onto a donkey for transport back to the house.

To prepare the pimento for sale, the berries had to be dried and carefully separated from any remaining small stems. We had a large, flat, rectangular concrete structure raised off the ground, with a smooth cemented surface where the green berries were laid out to dry. This drying platform, known locally in Jamaica as a "Ba-bi-cu," played an essential role in processing the pimento.

There were times, however, when some branches with pimento berries were overlooked during the harvesting, sometimes even intentionally. After the main harvesting was done, I would walk around the property to inspect the trees and check for any leftover berries. If I found any, I would carefully gather them for myself in a practice we called "skimming."

Because pimento was a valuable commodity, I was able to earn a considerable sum from selling the harvested berries. This newfound income allowed me to buy a few goats, which soon multiplied and provided me with a steady supply of milk. I began selling this milk to neighbours, further expanding my small business.

In addition to farming, I developed another skill: barbering. By the time I was about fifteen or sixteen, I had taught myself to cut hair. Some parents in the community began sending their children to my house for haircuts, and I earned pocket money from this side hustle. It became another source of income and a sign of the resourcefulness I had developed over the years.

Life in the countryside taught me to be self-reliant from a young age. Whether it was selling pimento berries, raising goats, cutting hair, or crafting kites, every small hustle shaped my sense of independence. Yet, alongside these practical skills, there was always a quiet but growing hunger for something more. An education that could open doors beyond the hills and farmlands of my youth. That hunger, fueled by my mother's persistence and my own ambitions, would soon lead me into classrooms where new possibilities awaited.

Easter was always one of the happiest times of the year for me, second only to Christmas. The holiday was marked by cherished traditions in Jamaica, where families would fly kites and enjoy the delightful treat of bun and cheese. To this day, I continue the tradition of having a bun and cheese every Easter.

From the age of fourteen, I became skilled at making and selling kites. I received numerous orders from parents who wanted kites for their children to fly on Good Friday and Easter Monday, the two days when kite flying was most popular. My talent for creating these kites made me a sought-after seller, and Easter became a busy and profitable time for me as I worked hard to meet the demand.

However, there was one Easter that was particularly heartbreaking for me. A pastor visited my church and told the congregation that flying kites was "an abomination to the Lord." Unfortunately, my mother, who was the decision-maker in our household, accepted this belief. My father didn't quite agree, but it was my mother's word that counted the most. That Easter was a very difficult time for me, as I had to give up something I loved: making, selling, and flying kites.

The following Easter, however, things changed. Whether it was the pastor's influence fading or my mother's change of heart, I was once again allowed to make and fly my kites. I didn't really care why it happened; I was just overjoyed to return to the hobby that had brought me so much joy in the past. To this day, I still make kites for my grandchildren and even fly one myself, continuing a tradition that has brought me happiness for years.

My days at Newstead Primary School

In Jamaica, sports play a significant role in the educational experience, with every school, ranging from basic schools and kindergartens to universities, hosting a Sports Day. This event is a full day dedicated to track and field competitions that draw large crowds, as students and families gather to cheer on their favorite athletes.

In Jamaican schools, students are organized into Houses, a tradition that was inherited from British colonial rule, which lasted for several centuries. The names of these Houses are often inspired by notable local figures or the names of flowers, reflecting the culture and heritage of the area. During Sports Day, these Houses compete against each other in various athletic events. To prepare for this day, each House would hold daily practice sessions after school, helping their athletes hone their skills and improve their performance.

As for me, I was an all-around athlete and earned the title of Champion Boy or Athlete of the Year at Newstead School. It's quite amusing, but my three sons also went on to achieve Athlete of the Year honors at their respective high schools, so I guess the athletic talent runs in the family!

In Jamaica, the typical school-leaving age for students attending primary and all-age schools was 16. If a student did not pass the "Eleven-Plus" exam, a critical scholarship test that determined eligibility for entrance into one of the limited numbers of high schools, their education would end at 16 years old, which was a lot more common in rural areas. Due to the fact that your formal education ceased at 16, some school-leaving students would seek to enter into a trade, training to become carpenters, mechanics, electricians, masons, and so on, while others might look for employment in the tourism industry, which was booming in the area where I lived.

In rural schools, there was a shortage of trained teachers, which made it much more difficult for students to pass the "Eleven-Plus" exam and gain access to high schools, especially compared to their peers in urban areas. However, over time, as more trained teachers were hired in rural schools, the success rates improved significantly.

When I reached the age of sixteen, I had a clear ambition: I wanted to become an electrician. It seemed like a reliable, well-paying job with clean work conditions, and I thought it would provide a solid future. Little did I know that my path would take me in different directions, but the foundation of hard work and ambition from those early years would stay with me.

Things took a positive turn when a dynamic young teacher named Winston Marsh became our principal. Full of energy and vision, he recognized the untapped potential in us 16-year-olds about to graduate, but with limited opportunities to further our education. At that time, Winston was a fresh, inspiring force, and today, he holds the title of Dr. Winston Marsh, a university lecturer in South Florida, with connections to institutions in Jamaica.

He saw something in us that we hadn't even realized. That we had the drive to pursue something greater, despite the barriers. I'm not entirely sure if he reached out to the Ministry of Education or if it was his initiative, but he managed to secure a program that allowed us to continue our education beyond the age of sixteen. This program was designed to prepare us for the Jamaica School Certificate (JSC) exam, which, while below the General Certificate of Education (GCE) offered by the University of

London and the University of Cambridge, was still a significant step for us. The GCE was a key high school-leaving exam in all Commonwealth countries, except for Canada.

I can vividly recall that there was a large utility room attached to the back of the main school building. This space was transformed into a makeshift classroom, where we, a small group of determined students, were set apart from the regular school population. Each one of us was committed to making the most of this opportunity. For me, that meant carrying my notebooks everywhere, even as I took my goats out to graze in the fields in the mornings and evenings. I spent late nights studying by the light of a kerosene lamp, its shade reading "Home Sweet Home." This hard work paid off. When the JSC exam results came out, I had passed all eight subjects I had taken.

CHAPTER 11

Dreams Beyond the Hills: My Road to Mico

By the time I was eighteen years old, I had earned the opportunity to apply for a pre-trained teaching position. I landed a job at a primary school in the hills of northeastern St. Ann, Jamaica, in a former bauxite mining town called Beechers Town. The commute was a challenge: I had to take a taxi from my home to Ocho Rios, a 20-minute drive, and then walk the remaining seven miles up the mountain to the school. Eventually, I managed to catch a ride with the milk truck driver from my district, but it meant waking up even earlier and sitting in his truck for hours as he made stops collecting milk cans from different farms along the way.

I stayed at Beechers Town Primary School for about six months before moving on to a new position at Exchange All Age School, which was only a 10-minute taxi ride away. This new job marked a turning point for me financially. I was now earning money, and I used it to help my mother, giving her some financial support. We also partnered in a small business venture, where we bought chicks, raised them to adulthood, and sold the chickens locally.

Looking back, I realize that this journey was transformative. The group of students who began this program with me, around thirty to forty in total, went on to achieve great things. Many of them became successful business leaders, teachers, principals, and entrepreneurs, and I feel proud to have been part of that legacy.

My first steps into the working world gave me not just a paycheck but a deeper hunger for growth. Supporting my family felt rewarding, yet each day I stood in front of the classroom, I realized I wanted to be more than just a local teacher, I wanted to reach my full potential. Conversations with friends, glimpses of life beyond my small town, and encounters with educated people showed me that there was a bigger world out there. My teaching job was just the beginning. My next goal was clear: to further my education and open the doors that once seemed too far away.

I grew up during a time when many of the friends I spent time with shared the same goal: to make something meaningful of our lives. We all understood that achieving this required obtaining a solid education, which became the foundation of our ambition. Although we were driven, there was some negativity from certain peers who didn't share our vision. They often labeled us as show-offs, but their opinions never bothered us.

Ocho Rios, a popular tourist town just fifteen minutes from my home, provided us with plenty of opportunities for exploration and inspiration. My friends and I often visited the beach, and on numerous occasions, we struck up conversations with tourists around our age. We were always fascinated and impressed by the fact that many of them were attending universities. These interactions further fueled our desire to pursue higher education, motivating us to strive even harder toward our goals.

Personally, I aspired to become a teacher, so I decided to sit for the entrance examination for Mico Teacher's College, one of the most renowned educational institutions in the Caribbean. I successfully passed the exam and was accepted into this prestigious institution, which had earned a reputation for excellence. Mico Teacher's College, now known as Mico University College, was not only the oldest teachers' college in the region but also a symbol of educational prestige. Founded in 1835 with a generous bequest from philanthropist Lady Mico, the college attracted students from across the globe, and I was proud to be among them.

In September 1972, I embarked on a transformative journey as I left home to attend Mico Teachers College. At just 18 years old, I was a country boy venturing into the unknown. Back then, going to college was a monumental achievement in my community, something only a select few accomplished. To mark this significant milestone, my mother hired a local minibus for the trip to Kingston, where the college was located. She made it a celebratory occasion, inviting a few of her closest aunts and friends to join. It was a moment of immense pride for her to see her son stepping into a world of opportunity.

Upon arriving on campus, I was greeted by a bustling scene. Hundreds of students and their families had gathered, many having traveled in a similar fashion as we did. Senior students, serving as volunteers, were present to help us settle in. The college had two male dormitories: Mills Hall and Principal Hall. Female students, however, were housed off-campus and shuttled to the college for classes. I was assigned to Mills Hall, where each room housed three students. A senior and two first-year students.

While college education itself was free, I needed to cover costs for books, clothing, and other essentials. Fortunately, I had saved money from my time working as a pre-trained teacher to handle these expenses.

This was my first experience living away from home, and while it was daunting, it was also exhilarating. I took great pride in letting my friends know I was now a college boy living in the bustling city of Kingston.

Mico College offered two distinct teaching programs: The Secondary Teaching Program and the Primary Teaching Program. Admission to the Secondary Program required a minimum of five GCE O-Level passes, while students like me, who had Jamaica School Certificate (JSC) qualifications or fewer GCE passes, were placed in the Primary Program. Upon graduation, students in the Secondary Program were assigned to secondary or high schools for internships, while those in the Primary Program were placed in primary or all-age schools.

As a first-year student, I encountered the tradition of "ragging," or hazing, imposed by second-year students. While most viewed it as a rite of passage, some seniors took it too far, creating lasting animosity. Being naturally defiant, I often resisted these unreasonable demands, which only brought additional challenges. One particularly humiliating task involved dressing in a jacket, shirt, and tie paired with shorts and running shoes to perform laps around the athletic track. Though I reluctantly complied to avoid further harassment, I found the entire ritual absurd.

Despite these challenges, my years at college were some of the most rewarding of my life. Living in the dormitory allowed me to forge lasting friendships and immerse myself in campus life. My chosen elective was Mathematics, as I was more comfortable with numbers than with reading. I considered myself an above-average student, managing to pass all my exams despite not having a traditional high school education.

Unlike many of my peers, I wasn't overly dedicated to studying. I avoided study groups and didn't spend hours poring over textbooks, as I was not a strong reader. Instead, I relied on my natural aptitude for problem-solving and my visual and hands-on learning style, which contributed to my success in Mathematics.

My creativity and resourcefulness often helped me stand out. In a child study assignment, where we were tasked with observing a child in their natural environment and drafting a report, I took an unconventional approach. While my classmates scrambled to observe real children in schools, I stayed in my dorm and fabricated a detailed report about an imaginary child. To my surprise, my report received one of the highest grades in the class.

Similarly, in an English Literature assignment requiring us to read a book and present a report, I created my own story instead. My fictional tale, *Sir Davis and the Lion*, captivated my classmates as I recounted the adventures of a young African boy who bravely fought a lion with a spear to save his village, ultimately earning the title of chief. The story earned me top marks and cemented my reputation as a storyteller.

Today, I continue to weave tales for my grandchildren, though they often catch on when I incorporate them into the stories. Still, storytelling remains one of my favorite ways to share lessons and entertain those I love.

CHAPTER 12

Finances, Freedom, and Heartbreak

At Mico College, teacher training spanned three years: two years of classroom-based learning and one year of internship at an assigned school. By September 1974, I had completed my two years of academic study and was ready for placement at a school to gain practical teaching experience. My assigned partner for the internship was Malcolm Johnson, whom we casually referred to as MalJo. Although we had not been friends during college, I had seen him around campus.

Our placement was at Inswood Primary School, located in a small district on the outskirts of Spanish Town, about 30 kilometers from Kingston. The school was nestled between expansive sugarcane fields that stretched on either side of the main road. Malcolm and I arranged boarding accommodation with a kind lady named Mrs. Brown, recommended by a previous intern. Her home in Spanish Town was perfect; it offered home-cooked meals and was conveniently located along a busy taxi route, making our 15-minute commute to the school both easy and affordable.

During the sugarcane harvest season, the fields around the school would be deliberately set ablaze to facilitate harvesting. The fires, though controlled, were a sight to behold. Thick black smoke billowed into the sky, often leaping across the main road to ignite the adjacent field. Motorists would come to a halt as the dense smoke obscured visibility. While the fires seemed perilously close to engulfing the district and the school, this practice had been carried out for decades without incident.

Our internship ended in July 1975, closing out the school year. With our training complete, we were free to apply to schools of our choice. Malcolm and I had become close friends by this time, so we decided to apply to the same school, McCauley Primary School, also located in Spanish Town. Spanish Town, the third-largest city in Jamaica after Kingston and Montego Bay, was historically significant as Jamaica's capital under Spanish rule.

The internship was more than just an academic requirement, it marked the transition from student life to professional life. As I walked out of Inswood Primary School for the last time, I carried with me not just teaching experience, but a newfound independence and lifelong friendships. Landing my first qualified teaching job felt like crossing an important threshold. Now, with a steady income, a growing social circle, and the freedom to build a life of my own, I was ready to embrace adulthood in every sense, both in the classroom and in the world beyond it.   With steady teaching jobs, we could afford to move out of our boarding accommodation. We rented a three-bedroom house just a few doors down the same street where we had stayed with Mrs. Brown. We invited a friend, Clement Burrell, to share the house. Clement had attended the College of Arts, Science & Technology (CAST), now known as the University of Technology. Together, we transformed the house into our own space, affectionately naming it "The Ranch."

As three young, fresh-out-of-college men, we embraced the vibrant lifestyle of the 1970s. Sporting large afros, bell-bottom pants, and colourful platform shoes, we exuded confidence. Our home became a social hub, frequently hosting friends and visitors, often of the opposite sex.

We formed a tight-knit group with fellow teachers and college alumni, including Greg Morris, who had been in the same year as us at Mico, and Lloyd Prince, a senior at the college. Lloyd, who taught at Spanish Town Secondary School, later earned his doctorate and became a lecturer at the University of the West Indies. Weekends were reserved for adventures. Lloyd's trusty old Volkswagen Beetle often carried us to parties in Kingston, Spanish Town, or the lush hills of St. Catherine. However, our favorite destination was the bustling resort town of Ocho Rios on the North Coast.

In Ocho Rios, we frequently visited Footprints, a popular nightclub that drew locals and tourists alike. We danced the nights away, often staying until the early morning before embarking on the hour-and-a-half drive back to Spanish Town. Occasionally, we befriended tourists vacationing in Ocho Rios and invited them back to The Ranch. These gatherings often extended to nights out in Kingston, adding an international flair to our already lively social life.

Life at The Ranch was a whirlwind of teaching, friendships, and unforgettable experiences. Looking back, it was a time of growth, joy, and camaraderie. A chapter that set the stage for the lifelong friendships and memories we cherish today.

Until this point in my life, I hadn't had a steady girlfriend. That changed during a holiday break when schools and colleges were closed. I happened to visit Mico College, which at the time was being used as a training facility for recent high school graduates participating in the National Youth Service (NYS) program. This initiative, introduced by Prime Minister Michael Manley, allowed young graduates to gain work experience and earn a modest salary, often in roles such as assistant teachers.

It was there that I met Elizabeth Belnavis, or "Betty" as she was affectionately called. She was an elegant, intelligent, and strikingly beautiful 18-year-old girl. I was about two years older than her, and from the moment I met her, I was captivated. Betty and I hit it off quickly, and soon enough, we were dating. Our relationship blossomed rapidly, and we began spending more and more time together.

However, there were challenges. Betty lived in Kingston while I was in Spanish Town, and since neither of us owned a car, we relied on buses to see each other. Despite the inconvenience, we made it work. Over time, I got to know her family well through my frequent visits to her home.

During this period, I was still clinging to my party-going lifestyle. But as my feelings for Betty deepened, I realized I was ready to leave that chapter of my life behind. I was in love with her and decided it was time to settle down.

Betty had started college by then, and I often visited her on campus. Everything seemed to be going well, at least from my perspective. But one day, completely out of the blue, Betty broke up with me. She didn't believe I was ready to commit to the life she envisioned for us. I was blindsided. As I rode the bus back home, tears filled my eyes. I had been so sure of my feelings, but in hindsight, I realized she had valid reasons for ending things.

Heartbroken, I fell back into my old partying lifestyle, trying to distract myself from the pain. But life has a way of throwing unexpected moments at you. One day, while walking down St. John's Road in Spanish Town, I encountered an experience that would change the course of my life forever.

CHAPTER 13

Moments That Shaped My Path

The moment that would forever change my life unfolded on a sunny and beautiful Friday evening. My friend Malcolm Johnson and I were walking up St. John's Road in Spanish Town after school, eagerly anticipating the weekend ahead. As we strolled, we noticed three strikingly beautiful white British women approaching from the opposite direction. Their appearance alone made them stand out; they didn't have the typical look or style of white Jamaicans, despite the presence of many in the area. Their attire marked them as newcomers, and we immediately recognized an opportunity to make an impression.

As I've mentioned earlier in this book, Malcolm and I believed we were quite the catch in those days, strutting around in our afros, bell-bottom pants, and platform shoes. There was no way we were going to let these ladies walk past without at least starting a conversation.

Here's how it went:

Malcolm: "Have you folks just moved into the area?"

Dena (the spokesperson): "Yes, we're expatriate teachers from England, working at St. Catherine High School."

Me: "Where are you staying?"

Dena: "At Mrs. Baxter's house, just down this street." (She gestured toward the house.)

Malcolm: "Oh, we're teachers too! We've just come from McAuley, the school down the road." **Me:** "Would you like us to show you around sometime? Maybe we could go to a movie and help you get familiar with the area."

Avril & Sue (enthusiastically): "Sure, we would love that!" **Dena:** (Silent but observant.)

The conversation continued for a bit, and we made plans to pick them up at a later date for the movie. However, when we arrived at their house, they changed their minds. Though disappointed, we decided to stay and chat, taking the opportunity to get better acquainted.

Over the next few weeks, as the women became more comfortable with us, we invited them to "The Ranch," our new two-bedroom apartment, which Malcolm and I had rented after Clement Burrell moved out. Knowing we needed backup, we roped in my cousin Luddy Lee. Luddy not only had transportation but also access to liquor, thanks to his well-off aunt, a businesswoman who owned several bars and restaurants in Spanish Town.

We were thrilled when the ladies accepted our invitation. The Ranch was ready: music was playing, and our signature red light on the porch was glowing. Malcolm and I had already decided who we would pursue; Malcolm would go for Avril, while I had my sights set on Sue, leaving Luddy to pair with Dena, the reserved and religious one.

When they arrived, Luddy made a beeline for Sue, leaving me free to approach Avril. Malcolm ended up chatting with Dena. The evening was electric. We danced, laughed, and sipped drinks late into the night. To cap it all off, I received a kiss from Avril, a moment I believe sealed our connection.

The women eventually moved into their own rental home near us, complete with a helper named Eileen and her adorable two-year-old son, Colin, whom they adored. Their home was a mere five-minute walk from our place, across the train tracks. I visited Avril often, but I wasn't her only admirer. Other suitors, including Dave, Marvin, Raymond, and a well-off supermarket owner, frequently competed for her attention. One persistent contender, Bobby, brought her boxes of ice cream, perhaps as a bribe or a token of affection. Luckily for me, Avril would hand the ice cream over to me, which Malcolm and I happily devoured at The Ranch.

What started as a casual flirtation quickly deepened into something more meaningful. As Avril and I grew closer, my career path was evolving too. The same streets where we first crossed paths soon led me to a new chapter, not just in love, but in professional life. When the opportunity arose to move into high school teaching, alongside Avril and our circle of friends, I seized it without hesitation. It felt like life was offering me a chance to grow, both personally and professionally, and I was ready to embrace it.

After a year of teaching, Malcolm and I decided to move on to new schools. He secured a position at Spanish Town Secondary, while I joined Avril, Sue, and Dena at St. Catherine High School as a Mathematics teacher. Teaching grades 7, 9, and 11, I found myself in the same professional environment as Avril, who taught Home Economics. Sue and Dena continued with Physical Education and Geography, respectively.

Fitting into the St. Catherine staff was easy. Many of my colleagues were acquaintances from Mico Teachers' College, including Junior Williams, George Foster, and Beryl McKay. The school operated on two campuses, junior and senior. Each with its own staff room where we prepared lessons and socialized between classes. With about 80 teachers on staff, the school was bustling, led by Principal Sister Pascal, a disciplined Catholic nun, and two vice principals: the stern Miss Anderson and the jovial Mrs. Fuller. I quickly built a great rapport, especially with Mrs. Fuller, who was also a family friend of my ex-girlfriend, Betty.

By this point, Avril and I had grown closer. Despite the competitions I had occasionally encountered, it deepened our bond, which I thought would one day lead to something extraordinary.

The junior staff room was by far the most popular gathering spot among teachers, primarily because it was frequented by the younger, more energetic staff. In contrast, the senior staff room often housed older teachers, many of whom had a reputation for being somewhat self-important and aloof.

Jamaicans have an undeniable love for celebrations, and this enthusiasm carried over into the culture at St. Catherine High. To kick off the new school year and foster camaraderie among the staff, parties were traditionally organized at the beginning of each term. These events served as opportunities for teachers to socialize and unwind outside the confines of the classroom.

As newcomers to the school, Avril, Dena, and Sue found themselves hosting one such party at their home, a large house that made it an obvious choice for the event. Their status as "newbies" left them with little room to refuse. Avril, eager to make the best of the situation, extended invitations to Malcolm and I, ensuring we would be part of the lively gathering.

The party was well attended, buzzing with laughter, music, and the clinking of glasses. Avril, perhaps emboldened by one drink too many, surprised me by walking over, settling herself on my lap, and planting a kiss on me. While her bold gesture was met with surprise, it carried unintended complications. She was unaware that I was dating another member of staff, and I was in the process of ending the relationship with her. The situation made her actions a bit awkward, as she did not anticipate the drama that followed. My memory of that evening was a bit dramatic; unbeknownst to Avril, my ex-girlfriend's sister, who was also attending the party and was just about ready to strangle me.

CHAPTER 14

My First Official Date with Avril

My first true date with Avril took place at the luxurious Sheraton Hotel in New Kingston. At the time, I didn't have a car, so I enlisted my landlord and his girlfriend to join us for the evening. He was more than happy to oblige, as he had spent many years in England and was eager to reminisce with someone from England. I had just begun my teaching career, and my salary as a first-year teacher was barely enough to cover my basic expenses. Avril, on the other hand, earned a significantly higher wage as an expatriate teacher, along with additional benefits like airfare and gratuity at the end of her contract.

Given my financial situation, I knew I could only afford a single drink at the hotel, so I convinced Avril to discreetly bring a flask of rum that I had purchased from the local store and tuck it into her handbag. She was initially reluctant but agreed. Once we arrived at the hotel and got settled, we ordered two rum and Cokes, along with an extra bottle of Coke. That night, Avril jokingly swore that she would break up with me the following day, but here we are, 48 years later, still together.

At the time, Malcolm and I were still living together, and we realized we needed some form of transportation. Pooling our resources, we managed to buy a used Ford Anglia. It wasn't the most reliable car, but it served its purpose. The car came equipped with four Mag rims, which, had we sold them at the time, would have fetched more money than the car itself.

We lived in a house that had a carport, with an iron gate at the end of the driveway. However, the gate was never locked because our landlord, who worked shifts, would occasionally come home at odd hours.

One night, as I was fast asleep, I heard someone softly calling my name. At first, I thought I was dreaming, but the voice persisted. Eventually, I woke up to realize it was my next-door neighbour, who was trying to alert me that my car had been pushed out of the carport and was being tampered with by a couple of thieves. Without thinking, I grabbed my machete and ran outside, chasing the thieves before they could hot-wire the car and make off with it.

Knowing that they might return, I quickly devised a simple but effective security system. I tied a string to the car's bumper, allowing it to rest flat on the ground, then ran it through my semi-closed window and attached it to my big toe. It worked like a charm. A few nights later, the thieves returned, and as soon as the string tugged, I was immediately alerted. Grabbing my machete, I charged out the door after them, watching as they scaled the fence in panic, as if they were fleeing from a lion chasing a deer.

It seemed like those guys must have really had their sights set on those Mag wheels, perhaps even stalking me, because one night, I stayed over at Avril's house. When I woke up the next morning and went outside to head home, my car was gone. I immediately reported the theft to the police, providing them with a detailed description of the car, but they were of little help. A few days later, however, a student from my school came forward and mentioned that they had seen my car sitting on blocks with all four wheels removed. When I informed the police of the car's location, one officer mentioned that he had passed by it but hadn't recognized it as the vehicle that had been reported stolen, even though I had given a very thorough description. It was incredibly frustrating and felt rather pitiful. After I managed to retrieve the car, it sat in my carport for some time because I didn't have the funds to get it back on the road.

CHAPTER 15

Avril's Parents' Trip to Jamaica

Avril's parents were planning their first visit to Jamaica, and she suggested that she would give me the money to repair the Ford Anglia so she could use it to drive them around the island. It seemed like a no-brainer to me; I agreed without hesitation. With her help, I bought out Malcolm's share of the car, and it ended up being a decision that worked out well for everyone involved.

I've always believed that if you aspire to be wealthy one day, it's important to start embodying the lifestyle of success. So, when my Ford Anglia was inoperable, I decided to invest in an old 1964 Mercedes-Benz SE for just $560. My cousin Rozzel, who was living with us in the new house we had rented and worked as a mechanic, helped me with some repairs, and I had the car repainted to give it a fresh, polished look. I absolutely loved driving that car, as it provided a sense of status and pride in Jamaica.

In 1976, Avril's parents arrived for their first visit to Jamaica. We decided to drive the Mercedes to Kingston's airport to pick them up. Avril was thrilled to have her parents visiting after so long. We loaded them into the car and set off for Spanish Town, a 30-kilometer journey. The drive was smooth, and Avril was eagerly chatting with her parents, catching up on all the news from back home. Everything was going well until we reached Spanish Town. As I turned the corner onto Avril's street, a loud bang erupted from beneath the car, and the vehicle came to a sudden stop, about a hundred feet from her driveway.

I quickly went out to investigate the source of the noise. Kneeling to inspect under the car, I discovered that one end of the driveshaft had fallen onto the ground, while the other end remained attached to the car. The rubber coupling that connected the driveshaft to the transmission had completely shattered. Despite the situation, with Avril and her parents, who were understandably exhausted after their long nine-hour flight from England, we managed to push the car into the driveway. It was a memorable moment, both frustrating and funny, considering how everything had seemed so perfect just moments earlier.

Avril's father, Maurice, was an enthusiastic and skilled cricketer who had spent many years playing for a local team in York, England. He was deeply passionate about the sport, and I had promised Avril that I would take him to a match at Sabina Park in Kingston, Jamaica, where England would be playing the West Indies in a Test series. Maurice, who was eager to experience live cricket in the Caribbean, would have been thrilled by the opportunity.

However, I soon found myself facing a major dilemma. My Ford Anglia, which I was relying on for transportation, was still in the garage being repaired, and the Mercedes-Benz was inoperable, parked on Avril's driveway. Left without a vehicle, I reached out to a friend who had an old Ford Prefect, a British-made car that predated the Ford Anglia by several years. While the Ford Prefect was an option, there was a catch. It lacked a starter motor. To get it going, I would need to perform a clutch/bump start.

For those unfamiliar with this method, a clutch/bump start can only be done on a manual transmission car and requires either an incline or someone pushing the vehicle. The process involves sitting in the car with the gearshift in second gear, the clutch engaged, and then releasing the clutch once the car reaches around 5 miles per hour. This action would start the engine.

Fortunately, I had a reliable backup in Junior Williams, one of my best friends, who was also an avid cricket fan. Junior and I had attended college together, and we were both teaching at St. Catherine High School. He agreed to accompany me to Sabina Park and serve as my "starter motor" if we couldn't find a suitable incline.

When we arrived at the stadium, Sabina Park was packed to capacity, and we were unable to secure seats together. There were only a few scattered individual seats, so Maurice ended up sitting in a section far from Junior and me. As I glanced over, I couldn't help but notice the contrast, here was Maurice, a small white man, surrounded by a sea of lively Jamaicans, all enjoying the match with food, drinks, and laughter.

Maurice seemed to embrace the festive atmosphere wholeheartedly. He was treated to generous servings of fried chicken and rice and peas, and the rum was flowing freely. As he always recounts, it was one of his best experiences in Jamaica, and he fondly recalls how well he was looked after by the locals.

After the match ended, we made our way to the car. This time, Junior didn't need to push the vehicle because I had managed to park the Ford Prefect on a small incline. I just rolled down the incline, popped the clutch, and pressed the gas pedal, and the engine roared to life.

With the car running, we headed back to Spanish Town, a journey that would normally take about 35 minutes. However, as we drove along the dual carriageway between Kingston and Spanish Town, the Ford Prefect suddenly started stuttering. I quickly assumed we were running out of gas. The fuel gauge wasn't working, but my friend had assured me we had enough to get to Kingston and back. I pulled over to the side of the road, and Maurice looked bewildered as to why we had stopped.

To my surprise, I discovered a piece of hose in the trunk, a tool my friend had used to siphon gas from generous passersby in case of an emergency. Junior, ever the resourceful companion, stood at the back of the car holding the hose aloft, signaling for help, while I popped the hood and pretended to attend to the problem, hoping to keep Maurice from catching on.

Maurice, puzzled, watched as I worked on the car. Coming from England, he was accustomed to fueling up at the first sign of a drop in the gas tank, so the idea of running out of fuel didn't even cross his mind. Luckily, our scheme worked. Amid the steady stream of cars passing by, one vehicle pulled over to help, none other than Avril's head of department at St. Catherine High. We siphoned some gas from her tank and were back on the road, continuing our journey home.

Maurice never misses an opportunity to share this memorable story, often recounting his experience of running out of gas and receiving help from a kind stranger. It remains one of his favorite tales from his time in Jamaica.

Since then, I've come a long way in terms of vehicles. Today, I own a Mercedes-Benz SL 550, a Jaguar F-Pace, a Jaguar XF, a

Jaguar XK8, and even a 1929 Mercedes-Benz SSK replica that I built. Looking back, I can't help but smile at the humble beginnings of those unforgettable adventures.

CHAPTER 16

The Unexpected Door to Concordia University

After two years of teaching, I began to question whether this was truly the career I wanted for the rest of my life. While I loved teaching, I quickly realized that it didn't provide the financial stability necessary for the comfortable lifestyle I envisioned. I found myself considering other career options that could offer greater earning potential.

To explore my options, I took on a job at Duff's Business College in Kingston, where I taught Mathematics to pre-business students. In addition to that, I started selling Britannica Encyclopedias to supplement my income. For those who may not know, this was a collection of hardcover books that provided comprehensive knowledge, which we now access with a quick search on Google. These ventures demanded long hours of hard work, but the extra money I earned wasn't substantial.

I began to entertain the idea of furthering my education, which could open the door to a career change. I started researching universities in the United States, hoping that I could work part-time to support myself through school. After some time, I applied to the University of Wisconsin, and to my delight, I was accepted. However, the annual tuition was $6,000 USD, a significant amount of money at the time. The university assured me that there were on-campus job opportunities to help cover the costs.

During this period, the Jamaican government, under Prime Minister Michael Manley, had introduced a student loan program for individuals pursuing studies abroad, provided the course they intended to take was not available at the University of the West Indies (UWI). Back then, UWI was the sole institution serving the Caribbean, and the competition for a place there was fierce, so the prospect of studying abroad became even more appealing.

In 1977, I began making serious plans to enroll at the University of Wisconsin. I knew the key to securing a student loan was reaching out to someone influential. I decided to contact Mr. Seymour Mullings, the Deputy Prime Minister of Jamaica, whom I had known personally for years. Mr. Mullings, a former land surveyor, was a friend of my father, who had entered politics. My father was a dedicated supporter during his campaign for Member of Parliament in our constituency.

I called Mr. Mullings and explained my intention to study at the University of Wisconsin, asking for his help in securing a student loan. He told me to reach out to him again when I was scheduled for the interview with the Student Loan Bureau, and that he would personally assist me with the process.

As luck would have it, one of the directors of the Student Loan Bureau happened to live on my street in Spanish Town. I had never really spoken to him, but we occasionally exchanged polite waves as he drove by. He was a family man with children,

71

and I often wondered what he thought of me. A young, carefree man with different women visiting me frequently. I pondered whether he saw me in a positive or negative light, given the nature of my lifestyle at the time.

Determined to make a more meaningful connection, I decided to casually approach him whenever I saw him standing at his gate. In our neighbourhood, the houses were all gated, and it was common for neighbours to stand at their gates and chat with passersby. This gave me the perfect opportunity to strike up a conversation and build a rapport with him.

With the student loan process well on its way, I also had other practical matters to consider, such as what to do with my 1964 Mercedes-Benz SE and my furniture. I decided to leave my furniture with my mother and let my brother Valin take care of my car. He ended up using it as a taxi, which worked out for both of us.

In hindsight, it seemed like everything was falling into place, and my future was taking shape. The next chapter of my life was within reach.

Just when I thought my path was set, life had a surprise waiting for me. One ordinary day, a casual conversation would alter the course of my future in the most unexpected way. A chance meeting with an old college friend would reveal an opportunity that seemed too good to ignore, and suddenly, the University of Wisconsin faded into the background, and a new, more attainable dream came into focus.

My initial plans to attend the University of Wisconsin were completely transformed when I unexpectedly ran into an old college mate, Craig Lewars, who was supervising O-Level exams at St. Catherine's High School. Craig had been a senior at Mico

Teacher's College when I was a junior student there, and I had always thought of him as a really cool guy. At the time, he was studying at Concordia University in Montreal, Canada, and had come back home on university break. After many years of teaching in Canada, Craig is now retired and living in Costa Rica.

During our conversation, I shared my plans to attend the University of Wisconsin, but I expressed my concerns about the high cost of tuition. It was a jaw-dropping moment for me when he explained that as an international student, he was paying only $750 CAD per year, the same tuition rate as Canadian students. I was stunned. I stood there, mouth agape, as I reflected on the enormous difference between that amount and the much higher fees I would have had to pay at the University of Wisconsin. I was completely flabbergasted.

At the time, I was also in a committed relationship with Avril, and I immediately went to see her to share the exciting news. She was overjoyed for me, and we both started to discuss the possibility of me pursuing this new opportunity. My previous plans now seemed irrelevant, and I was eager to take the next step. I grabbed a pen and paper and wrote a letter to Concordia University, expressing my interest in attending the university.

Within a week, I received a response from the university, which included application forms and detailed instructions on what documents I needed to submit. I quickly filled out the forms, attached all the necessary paperwork, sealed the envelope, and sent it off to the university with a sense of hope and anticipation.

As the weeks went by without hearing from them, I began to feel increasingly anxious. Normally, the university would respond quickly, but the silence was unnerving. During this time, Avril and I continued to enjoy our weekends together, often making trips to the north coast of Jamaica, to places like Ocho Rios.

One weekend, after returning from one of these trips, I was greeted with a letter from Concordia University. My heart began to race as I wondered if this was the moment I had been waiting for. Should I open it now? Was I accepted or rejected?

I finally mustered the courage to open the letter, my hands trembling. The first line read, "Thank you for submitting your application," and my immediate thought was that they were simply acknowledging my submission out of courtesy, and I had been rejected. But I forced myself to keep reading. "We are pleased to inform you that you have been accepted to Concordia University," it said. I had to read it again to make sure I hadn't misinterpreted the words.

Overwhelmed with joy, I rushed to Avril's house to share the wonderful news. She was just as excited as I was. To celebrate, she brought out the gin and tonic, a staple at their house. And we toasted to this new chapter in my life. It was a moment of pure happiness, and I couldn't wait to begin this new journey at Concordia University.

CHAPTER 17

Crossing Borders, Building Family

In the summer of 1977, with schools on break for the summer holidays, Avril, Sue, and Dena were preparing to leave Jamaica. They had come to the island two years earlier on a teacher's work visa, which had now expired. It was time for them to return to England.

During their time in Jamaica, Sue had met a gentleman named Tim Hill in 1976. Tim, a Financial Controller, worked at a hotel on the north coast of Jamaica called Club Caribbean (now known as Decameron). Sue had decided to move in with Tim on the North Coast, while Dena was heading back home to England.

Avril and I had discussed the possibility of her accompanying me to Canada, and as a result, she decided to move in with me. I was sharing a three-bedroom house with Malcolm and a childhood friend, Charles Russell, who had recently graduated from the College of Science and Technology, where he studied to be a pharmacist.

Having Avril move in with me served me very well, as I had more availability of food. Before she moved in, a tin of corned beef, a staple means of protein in Jamaica, would make me three dinners, complemented with a plate of steamed white rice. But now I was getting a whole tin of corned beef with other nutritious food. As I mentioned before, my teacher's salary was so little, it was spent before I even got my pay cheque.

When Avril's parents, Maurice and Mary Smith, visited her in Jamaica, we were not yet in a serious relationship. It wasn't until after their return to England that Avril and I grew closer, and our relationship took a more serious turn. So, when Avril informed them in a letter that she would be traveling to Canada with me, there was no response for over three months.

Finally, a letter arrived, explaining the delay. They had been reflecting on how best to respond. While Avril and her sister Rozzie were raised to believe that all races should be treated equally and without discrimination, her parents expressed concern about how their neighbours might perceive the relationship. They were also disappointed that Avril had not introduced me as her boyfriend during their visit to Jamaica, as our relationship had only truly developed after they had returned to England.

Over time, however, Avril's parents became the most wonderful in-laws anyone could ask for. When we got together, which happened often, I was always treated with kindness and respect. Mary would go out of her way to prepare my favorite desserts, making me feel incredibly welcome and cherished.

While Avril's parents initially had their reservations about our relationship, time, understanding, and shared moments began to soften those early concerns. As the years unfolded, not only did they welcome me into their family, but I formed a special bond with Maurice. One built on respect, curiosity, and admiration. It was through countless conversations, especially his incredible war stories, that I came to deeply appreciate the remarkable life he had lived and the extraordinary family I had become part of.

I've always had a fascination with war stories, and Maurice, my father-in-law, was undoubtedly the best person to talk to, having flown both the British Spitfire and the American Mustang during World War II. One of the most captivating stories he shared with me was about the time he was shot down over Yugoslavia. He was on a bombing mission targeting German forces when he received an unexpected radio message. The message told him that a convoy of German trains filled with military personnel, ammunition, and equipment was in the area. The radio operator informed him that the convoy was unarmed and instructed him to bomb it with everything he had. However, unbeknownst to the operator, the convoy was, in fact, fully armed.

Maurice explained that had he known the convoy was armed, he would have taken a different approach. Instead of following the convoy directly, he would have crisscrossed above it, releasing bombs from multiple angles. But at that moment, he followed the line of the train, dropping his bombs along its path. Suddenly, there was a violent jolt, and his engine was hit. He quickly climbed as high as he could, trying to distance himself from the enemy, but the engine eventually gave out.

With no other choice, Maurice ejected from the plane. However, his parachute became tangled with the tail of the aircraft as he descended. When the plane flipped, the parachute was freed, and he was able to glide safely to the ground. He landed on a mountain in Yugoslavia, where he noticed bear tracks nearby. Cautiously, he drew his pistol and followed the tracks, which eventually led him to a farmer working in his field at the base of the mountain. To Maurice's relief, the farmer turned out to be an ally of the British forces. The farmer helped him contact the British, who then came to retrieve him.

Afterward, Maurice was sent home for a week to recover and see his fiancée, Mary. When he showed up at her door, she fainted, as it had been reported that he had been shot down and presumed dead. She was convinced she was seeing a ghost. Remarkably, within a week, Maurice was back in the cockpit, flying sorties over Yugoslavia once again.

Maurice gave my eldest son, Mark, his wings from his flight jacket, which we now have proudly displayed in a frame along with a newspaper article documenting the incident of him being shot down and surviving. I also have a copy of his logbook, preserving the memories of a truly extraordinary man.

Just before the publication of this book, my nephew, Jason Francis, was researching Spitfires and made a fascinating discovery: out of the 20,351 Spitfires ever built, only 80 remain in existence today. Even more remarkably, the very last Spitfire that Maurice had flown was still operational at the Duxford Museum and Airfield in England, just a short distance from where he lived.

Avril and her sister Rozzie had the rare privilege of sitting in the cockpit of that historic aircraft, experiencing a poignant connection to their father's past. It was a deeply emotional moment for both of them.

CHAPTER 18

Farewells and Firsts: Leaving Home, Finding New Horizons

When Avril and I first began dating, she was a heavy smoker, and I absolutely hated it. At parties, she would pass me her cigarettes to keep in my pocket, since she didn't have any. I would distribute them, one by one, to the other smokers, and by the end of the evening, I was known as the go-to person for a cigarette at these gatherings. Ironically, despite never having smoked a cigarette or marijuana in my entire life, I became the unofficial distributor of cigarettes at these parties.

One evening, after I returned home from my part-time teaching job at Duff's Business College in Kingston, I found Avril sitting on the veranda, looking as beautiful as ever, wearing a pair of very short shorts and smoking a cigarette. She greeted me with a smile and, in a calm but resolute tone, declared that it was her last cigarette. True to her word, she never smoked again after that day.

Avril and I often visited Sue and Tim at their home in Runaway Bay on the north coast of Jamaica. We also spent time at Club Caribbean, where Tim worked as the financial controller. As we prepared to leave Jamaica, we decided to make one last trip to Negril. During that visit, Sue joined us for a few days at the hotel, but after she left, Avril and I rented a small, self-contained cottage on a hill near the famous Rick's Café. It was here that I proposed to Avril.

While in Negril, my friend George Foster, whom I had attended college with and who was also teaching at St. Catherine High School, arranged for us to meet his brother, John Foster. John, who had lived in Montreal and attended Mico College and Concordia University, turned out to be an invaluable contact, as we didn't know anyone in Montreal at the time.

John Foster was incredibly kind and generous. He would regularly pick us up on weekends and take us to various parties he attended. His hospitality played a significant role in helping us settle into life in Montreal.

Those last few months in Jamaica felt like a gentle farewell tour. Spending time with friends, sharing moments with Avril, and making those final memories in the place that shaped us. Yet as much as we tried to hold on to the comforts of home, a new journey was calling. And before we knew it, we were boarding a plane, leaving behind the familiar sounds of the island for the unfamiliar chill of Canada. Little did we know, the days ahead would be filled with both awe and adjustment as we stepped into a world vastly different from the one we had known.

On August 16, 1977, the same day Elvis Presley passed away, Avril and I boarded a plane at Norman Manley International Airport in Kingston, Jamaica, embarking on a journey toward an uncertain future. We were filled with anticipation, excitement, and a bit of trepidation. Our destination was Toronto, Canada, and upon landing at Pearson International Airport, we were picked up by my cousin Ray Llewellyn, who had come to welcome us.

At that moment, our entire world consisted of just two suitcases and a box of LP records. While I had already secured a spot at Concordia University, Avril's future was much more uncertain. She had entered Canada on a four-week visiting visa, and the big question loomed: would she be able to obtain a work permit to stay, or would she be forced to return to England after her visa expired?

This was my very first flight, and as the plane ascended, my eyes were fixed on the window. I marveled at the sight below. I had never seen Jamaica in such a way. My beautiful island, where it is always sunny. From above, the landscape appeared even more majestic, with the lush green mountains reaching toward the sky and the vibrant turquoise ocean stretching out beneath me. It was hard to believe that I was leaving such a paradise behind. I had spent many days swimming in those turquoise waters, and the idea of leaving all that for a cold land, as described by those who had worked on Canadian farms, seemed daunting. Canada, they said, was cold, and its people spent most of their winters indoors to escape the chill.

I reassured myself that this was only temporary. Once I completed my studies, I would return to the warmth of my homeland. But for now, the unknown awaited me.

Upon arriving at Pearson International, Ray, who had been living in Canada for four years after his mother, my Aunt Pearl, had sponsored him and his siblings, was there to meet us. We had grown up like brothers in Jamaica, and now he was ready to show us his new home country.

As we stepped outside the terminal, preparing to enter Ray's car, I felt a chill in the air that caught me off guard. With a puzzled look, I turned to him and asked why the air conditioning was set so low. Smiling, Ray chuckled and explained, "That's not the air conditioner. It's the weather. It's cold outside." As I looked up, I noticed the stars shining brightly in the sky, and it finally dawned on me that I wasn't indoors. I was experiencing the cool Canadian night air for the first time. It was a stark contrast to Jamaica, where the temperature never dropped below 60 degrees Fahrenheit. I then realized this was the beginning of a new chapter in my life, one that would come with new challenges, new experiences, and new memories.

I spent a week staying with Ray and his wife Alice, who graciously took me around to see my two aunts, Aunt Pearl and Aunt Vash. One of the highlights was when they took us to Honest Ed's, a legendary discount store in Toronto, known for being one of the biggest of its kind in the city, if not in all of Canada. It was an overwhelming experience, with its bargain prices and endless rows of items. After that, my aunts treated us to a trip to the Canadian National Exhibition (CNE), a beloved annual event that marks the end of summer. This carnival-style festival offers a variety of entertainment, rides, games, food stalls, exhibits, and even an air show. The CNE runs from the third Friday in August to Labor Day each year and is considered a tradition for many Ontarians, passed down through generations, drawing visitors from all over the region.

Later in the week, Avril and I decided to take a trip to Niagara Falls. We hopped on a bus in Toronto for a day trip, and when we arrived, the view of the falls was nothing short of breathtaking. It was the most spectacular sight I had ever seen. We walked down to the Canadian side of the falls, which offered the most magnificent vantage point. The area was bustling with people; hundreds gathered around the barricades near the falls, while others relaxed on the grass in the park, enjoying a live rock band. We stood there for a long time, marveling at the view, taking in the grandeur of the falls, and noticing people walking down a hill toward the water for a closer look.

Curious to get even closer, I noticed a long bridge in the distance, where several people were crossing to the other side. I suggested to Avril that we follow them, so we made our way onto the bridge and joined the crowd in crossing over. Once on the other side, we took in the sights, and after a while, we decided to head back. But as we approached the bridge to return to Canada, a uniformed officer stopped us. He asked for our identification, and when we explained that we didn't have driver's licenses and our passports were back at my aunt's house in Toronto, he seemed skeptical.

"How did you get over here?" he asked. I explained that we had simply walked over with the other visitors, as no one had stopped us when we crossed earlier.

The officer seemed to hesitate and then called for a colleague to ask us the same questions again. I repeated that we didn't have our IDs with us and told them we had just arrived in Toronto a few days earlier and were heading to Montreal for university. After a brief conversation between the officers, they decided to let us pass and return to Canada. I guess they either saw the sincerity in our responses or perhaps realized we were simply naïve tourists. We walked back through the bridge without further incident, wondering if perhaps the US Customs officer had simply nodded off when we passed through to the American side earlier.

We spent the rest of the week in Toronto, visiting Aunt Pearl, Aunt Vash, Ray, and several other cousins who had migrated to

Canada. It was a wonderful and memorable trip, with cherished moments spent with family, exploring the sights and sounds of the city.

CHAPTER 19

New Beginnings in Montreal

Our journey to Montreal began with a flight from Pearson International Airport in Toronto to Mirabel International Airport. Once we landed, we hailed a taxi and asked the driver to take us to the nearest motel to Concordia University, as that was where I would soon begin my studies. The driver took us to a modest motel located on Saint Jacques Street (Rue Saint Jacques), where the nightly rate was $22. While it served our immediate need for accommodation, we realized it would be too expensive for us to stay there long-term.

Determined to find a more affordable option, we spent the following day walking along Saint Jacques Street. Thankfully, we found another motel nearby that charged $17 per night. It wasn't luxurious, but it was within our budget, and we were relieved to have a temporary solution while searching for a more permanent place to live.

The next day marked the start of registration at Concordia University. Avril and I walked to the registration center, which was set up in the university's massive gymnasium. The process was impressively organized, with tables arranged alphabetically by surnames to streamline the registration. I received a course outline booklet, which provided an overview of the programs and courses available.

Initially, I planned to enroll in the Social Science program. This decision was somewhat vague and unmotivated; I had been a teacher and thought I wanted to continue working with people, or perhaps I just wanted to earn a degree and figure out my career path later. However, as I browsed through the course listings, Avril noticed something intriguing. She pointed out a program in the Engineering Department called Computer Science and suggested that I consider it.

At first, I dismissed the idea, thinking I wouldn't be qualified for an engineering-related program. However, Avril reminded me of my Mathematics background, and together, we started exploring the program further. We learned that I could major in Computer Science and minor in another field, or I could opt for a Double Specialization in Computer Science and Mathematics. The latter option was particularly appealing, as it combined my interest in math with a practical and emerging field like computer science.

The only drawback was that the Double Specialization was a four-year degree program, while most other programs were three years. This made me pause and reflect on the implications. At 23 years old, I was already considered a mature student, and completing a four-year program would mean I'd graduate at 27. Back then, many people my age were already married and raising children. Starting a family would have to wait if I chose this path.

After much discussion and deliberation, Avril and I decided that pursuing the four-year Double Specialization in Computer Science and Mathematics was the right choice. It was a significant commitment, but the combination of my skills and interests made it a logical and exciting step forward.

After finalizing my degree program and selecting my courses, the next task was to find an apartment. The following day, we picked up a copy of the *Montreal Gazette* and began our apartment hunt. Our first stop was a side street off Saint Jacques, where we checked out a one-and-a-half (1½) apartment. This layout included a bedroom, a living room, a bathroom, and a small kitchen, priced at $350 per month. However, that was a bit beyond our budget.

Undeterred, we explored several more options, but none seemed to suit our needs. Eventually, we came across another one-and-a-half apartment on Saint Jacques for $250 per month, which felt more comfortable and within our price range. The bedroom was bright and airy, thanks to its access to an open balcony shared with neighbouring apartments. Unfortunately, the living room and kitchen were darker, as they lacked natural light, but the overall space was cozy enough for us.

One of the apartment's highlights was the balcony. From there, we had a view of Highway 2&20 about a mile away, nestled in a gully. We could also see the intricate interchange leading to the Ville-Marie Expressway into downtown Montreal, the Champlain Bridge to the South Shore, and the Décarie Expressway. I particularly enjoyed sitting on the balcony, watching the steady flow of traffic, a simple yet satisfying pastime.

The apartment came with basic furnishings, including a bed and a sofa, but we needed kitchen supplies. After some shopping, we also added a used record player for the LP records I had brought with me. Without a television, entertainment options were limited, so I revisited the store where I'd purchased the record player. There, I found a massive black-and-white television that weighed at least 100 pounds, priced at just $35. Getting it home was a challenge, as the store was not on the bus route. Determined, I balanced the TV on my head and walked nearly two miles back to the apartment.

With our kitchen equipped, music playing on the record player, and the black-and-white TV set up, we finally felt settled in. Life was simple but comfortable, and we were ready to embrace this new chapter.

As I settled into my studies and we adjusted to our modest but cozy apartment, there was still one looming uncertainty: Avril's future in Canada. With her visitor's visa quickly running out, we knew we had to act fast. Just as we had done to find our home, we turned once again to the Montreal Gazette, determined to secure not only a job for Avril but also a way for her to stay and build her own new beginning in Montreal. We found ourselves in a challenging situation, figuring out how to secure a way for Avril to stay in Canada before her visa expired. Time was running out, and the pressure to find a solution grew. Once again, we turned to the *Montreal Gazette*, scouring the job listings for an opportunity that could provide her with a visa and allow her to work in the country.

After days of searching, Avril landed a job with a young couple who had a two-year-old daughter. They were looking for a nanny to care for their little girl. The mother worked as a buyer for a high-end store in Montreal, which required her to travel frequently to Hong Kong. While I can't recall the exact details of the father's occupation, I do remember he drove a Corvette, and the family lived in one of Montreal's more affluent neighbourhoods. They were a kind and welcoming family who treated Avril very well. The only drawback to this job was the commute; she had to take two buses to get to their home, which was both time-consuming and inconvenient.

Eventually, Avril found another job, this time with a family that had two young daughters. Their mother, Ann, worked as a physiotherapist, while the father, Richard, was an IT professional who occasionally lectured at Concordia University. This family was also warm and respectful, making her feel comfortable and valued in her role. Additionally, the commute to their home was significantly easier, requiring only one bus. Avril later purchased a second-hand bicycle, which made the journey to work even more manageable and allowed her to enjoy the fresh air and scenic rides through the city.

These experiences not only helped Avril establish herself in Canada but also introduced her to two wonderful families who appreciated her dedication and care. Each job came with its own challenges and rewards, shaping her journey and helping her build a new life in Montreal.

CHAPTER 20

Learning, Freezing, and Finding My Way

Concordia University is composed of two distinct campuses: the Loyola campus, located in the western part of Montreal, and the Sir George Williams campus, situated in the heart of downtown Montreal. These two institutions merged in 1974, forming what is now known as Concordia University.

The Loyola campus, established in 1896, boasts a historic charm with its expansive green spaces and older buildings. Most of my classes took place here until my final year, when I transitioned to the downtown Sir George Williams campus. This campus, in contrast, is a modern high-rise building, towering in the center of the city, with multiple floors offering a bustling urban atmosphere. Thankfully, shuttle buses ran between the two campuses, making travel between them convenient.

When the new semester began, the campus was filled with students returning from their holidays. The first week was typically spent socializing, purchasing textbooks, and figuring out where each class would be held. Textbooks were notoriously expensive, but the savvy students knew they could find used copies from others who had taken the same courses the previous year, often for half the price of a new one.

Being someone who was careful with my money, I might have been considered frugal, or some would even call it cheap. When I couldn't find a used book, I would buy a new one from the bookstore, take it to a nearby photocopy shop, have them photocopy and bind it, and then return the original book to the store for a refund. I wasn't the only one doing this, as many students were using the same strategy to save money.

The Loyola campus also had several student lounges, one of which offered coffee, snacks, and music. One afternoon, as I sat at a table having a cup of coffee, a group of fellow students, both guys and girls, joined me and began placing small, compressed cube-like objects on the table. They lit the cube with a cigarette lighter, and as soon as the cube ignited, a familiar scent filled the air, and I quickly recognized what it was. Though I had never seen these cubes before, I knew it was ganja/marijuana. Back in Jamaica, I had seen people smoke marijuana, but it was always in rolled paper or in a pipe, never in this cube form.

The group was passing a straw among themselves, inhaling the vapor, and they tried to offer it to me. I politely declined, explaining that I didn't use drugs. To my surprise, they were astounded that I, coming from Jamaica, didn't partake in smoking marijuana. In Jamaica, marijuana use was often frowned upon, and it was primarily associated with the Rastafarian culture. A group that faced significant discrimination. The situation highlighted the contrasting perceptions of marijuana use between my home country, Jamaica, and the campus culture at Concordia.

Concordia University attracted hundreds of international students from all over the world, likely due to its affordable tuition fees. I vividly remember being in a class that had students from thirty-five different countries. As the weeks went by, I began to forge friendships with many of these foreign students, each with their unique backgrounds and experiences. Among them, the Caribbean student community was notably large. What struck me at the time was that many of these international students, including those from Jamaica, came from well-off families. I was one of the few exceptions, but that didn't matter. Despite our differences in background, we all became good friends, united by the shared experience of studying abroad.

University life quickly became a whirlwind of new experiences, but it wasn't just the classrooms that tested me, it was everything outside of them, too. From grappling with unfamiliar academic subjects to navigating friendships in a multicultural environment, every day brought something new to overcome. But perhaps the most shocking lesson of all wasn't in a textbook, it was braving my first Canadian winter, an experience that would humble me more than any exam ever could.

My academic journey at Concordia began with a demanding mix of courses, including Physics, Mathematics (covering topics like Statistics, Equations, Transportation, Calculus, Proofs, Splines, Chains, Rings), various Computer Programming languages (such as Assembly, FORTRAN, Pascal, and COBOL), Chemistry, and several elective courses. As I've mentioned earlier in this book, I had never attended high school, and the subjects I encountered in my university courses were not part of the Teacher's Certificate program I completed at Mico College. Because of this, I faced a significant disadvantage. Many of the concepts in these subjects would have been introduced during high school, making them much harder for me to grasp at the university level.

I struggled in the beginning with some mathematics courses, as I was not exposed to them while I was in teachers' college. I constantly found myself asking my professors what I feared were basic questions. Ones that I should have already known the answers to. One day, after a particularly challenging Math class, Dr. Bedford, my professor for the course, a kind older gentleman who had taught high school before transitioning to university-level teaching, noticed my difficulties. After class, he invited me to his office and said, "I can see that you've missed out on some foundational theories." He generously lent me a book that explained key mathematical concepts like Sine, Cosine, Tangents, Derivatives, Integration, and Transformation. It was an invaluable resource that helped me catch up. I had to work much harder than most of my peers, but my perseverance paid off. In the end, I earned an "A" in Calculus 101, and I couldn't have been happier with the outcome.

Just as I was beginning to find my footing inside the classroom, a whole new challenge awaited me beyond campus walls. While conquering complex equations and unfamiliar subjects had been mentally taxing, nothing quite prepared me for what was next. My first brutal encounter with the infamous Canadian winter.

Montreal's winters were an absolute shock to my system, especially considering I had come from Jamaica, where the temperature hardly ever dropped below sixty-five degrees Fahrenheit. The cold was unlike anything I had ever experienced. I lived on Saint Jacques Street, which ran parallel to Sherbrooke Street, about a mile away. Loyola Campus was located on Sherbrooke, and to catch the bus there, I would walk along Wilson Street from my apartment, passing beneath the train tracks, until I reached Sherbrooke.

It was November when the temperatures began to plummet, and I still hadn't prepared for the harsh winter. I was still wearing my flimsy running shoes, which, at that time, were nothing like the high-performance Nike or Reebok brands we have now. One day, Avril and I were browsing in a shoe store, and she suggested that I buy a pair of winter boots. When she showed me the options, I was stunned. They looked like the kind of boots farm workers who went to work in Canada wore. I couldn't imagine myself wearing those, especially since we used to joke about how odd those boots looked on the farm workers who returned from the U.S. and Canada. I flat-out refused to buy them.

I had no idea what awaited me. One evening, I went to class when the weather was still bearable. I had gotten used to the chill by then, wearing a warm jacket and thick socks that kept my feet comfortable. But when class ended that night, the weather had taken a severe turn. The wind howled, and snow whipped through the air like a hurricane. Cars, buses, trucks, and people were all slipping and sliding everywhere. It was my first time experiencing such intense cold and snow.

I had to wait for the bus, but due to the storm, everything was at a standstill. The bus was almost an hour and a half late. By the time I finally got on, my feet were in agony. The pain was so unbearable that I thought they might fall off. What normally would have been a 25-minute trip back to my apartment took almost an hour and a half. When I finally got off the bus, I limped home, my feet throbbing with every step.

Once I got inside, the pain was so intense that I was desperate for relief. I ran some hot water and soaked my feet, but it only made things worse. The pain escalated, and I cried like a child.

The next day, I turned to Avril and said, "Let's go get those farm workers' boots." I was finally ready to face the harsh reality of Montreal's winters.

Despite the brutal introduction to winter, I was starting to feel more at home at the university. I met several students and made good friends, including Bob McAlister and Jimmy Tan, both of whom were in my program. Bob, a Montreal native, lived within walking distance of Loyola, while Jimmy was from Malaysia. We became fast friends, and over the next four years, our bond grew. I also got to know Bob's parents, Sister Lynne, and his fiancée Heather (now his wife). I attended Bob and Heather's wedding and have kept in touch with Heather and Lynne since.

CHAPTER 21

Love, Friendship, and the Unexpected Turns of Life

Avril and I had planned to get married in England on May 20, 1978, and, fortunately, we didn't have much to organize. Avril's parents and her sister, Rozzie, took care of everything in England; all we had to do was show up. Avril, who was a skilled Home Economics teacher, took on the task of creating her own wedding dress and the bridesmaids' dresses, showcasing her incredible talent for sewing.

We flew into London Gatwick Airport, where Rozzie and her husband, Vic, picked us up and took us to York in northern England, where Avril's parents lived. Avril's niece, Rachel, and my cousin Blossom's daughter, Pauline, were the bridesmaids for the day.

For my best man, I chose my cousin Luddy Lee, who had been part of the eventful night when we first met Avril, Sue, and Dena in Spanish Town. Luddy had since married an English-born woman of Jamaican descent and settled in England.

The wedding was attended by around sixty guests, including Avril's college friends and some of my cousins, who traveled from London to join us. Unfortunately, my mother couldn't attend the ceremony as she lived in Jamaica, and neither of us could afford the airfare for her to travel to England.

I had made arrangements with Avril's cousin, Malcolm Smith, to meet my cousin and best man, Luddy, at the train station. I had given Malcolm a detailed description of Luddy, what he would be wearing, and where he would be standing to help him recognize him.

On the morning of the wedding, Malcolm went to pick up Luddy, but much to his surprise, there was no sign of him. Assuming Luddy hadn't recognized him based on my description, Malcolm started asking every Black man who stepped off the train if they were Luddy. After a thorough search, he returned without him. As a result, Rozzie's husband, Vic Sims, stepped in to take the role of my best man.

The wedding ceremony itself was held in a historic church, one that, as I recall, may have been bombed during World War II by the Germans. The reception followed at The Three Cups, a pub that had been a favorite of Maurice's for many years. After the pub celebration, we returned to Maurice and Mary's house, where a marquee had been set up in the backyard. This was where the neighbours and other well-wishers who couldn't attend the ceremony or reception gathered for drinks and a bit of socializing.

For our honeymoon, we had booked a stay at the King's Hotel in London. However, we only stayed there for a couple of nights as it was quite expensive, and we then moved to my cousin Blossom's apartment. During this time, I caught up with Luddy and learned that he had gambled away the money for his train fare on a horse and lost it all. I couldn't help but chuckle to myself, thinking that some things never change; he had been a notorious gambler back in the days at the Caymanas Park racetrack in Spanish Town, Jamaica.

During our trip, we had the wonderful opportunity to visit some of Avril's friends and some of my relatives, while also exploring the country's rich culture and history. Our journey was filled with unforgettable moments, blending personal connection with exciting sightseeing adventures.

While staying in London, we made it a point to visit some of the city's most iconic landmarks. We marveled at the bustling energy of Piccadilly Circus, walked across the historic London Bridge, and admired the grandeur of Buckingham Palace. Each destination was unique, and collectively, they gave us a glimpse into London's vibrant character and historical significance. Our time in the capital was nothing short of fantastic. Back in York, a historic city, we joined a guided tour to explore its charming, narrow streets, which are paved with traditional cobblestones and exude a timeless atmosphere. The city is surrounded by an impressive medieval wall, complete with a grand entrance gate that adds to its old-world charm. York's beauty, combined with its rich history, made our visit there an enchanting experience.

After our whirlwind wedding in England and brief honeymoon in London, reality quickly pulled us back to Montreal and university life. The joy of starting married life was accompanied by the excitement of a new academic year, and soon, old friendships began to weave their way back into our story in the most unexpected ways.   It was September 1978, and I had just completed my first year at Concordia University when Malcolm Johnson, my close friend from Spanish Town, received his acceptance to the same university. Having lived together in Spanish Town for many years and shared countless experiences, it felt only natural to welcome him into my life in Montreal. Avril and I agreed to let Malcolm stay with us temporarily until he could find his footing and arrange more permanent accommodation.

However, just a week later, we received a surprise call from Clement Burrel, another longtime friend from Spanish Town. Burrel, who had been part of our shared rental house back home, announced that he would also be joining us at Concordia. His news came as a complete shock; I had no idea he had even applied to the university. Clement Burrel was a dreamer, a man with big ideas but often limited by financial constraints. I vividly recall how he once envisioned building a shopping mall in Spanish Town long before anyone else thought it was feasible. Ironically, about a decade later, a mall was constructed on the very spot he had identified for his ambitious project, proving his vision was ahead of its time.

With Burrel's arrival, our small one-bedroom apartment suddenly became home to four adults. While the situation was cramped, we managed to make it work, knowing it was only temporary. Within a couple of weeks, Malcolm and Burrel secured their own apartment within walking distance of Loyola Campus. To their surprise, their new living arrangement included sharing the house with another couple, who they later discovered were gay. This revelation caused tension, particularly for Burrel, whose views were shaped by his Jamaican upbringing, where homosexuality was not accepted. In Jamaica at the time, gay people were derogatorily referred to as "Batty Men" and faced widespread discrimination and even violence. Although attitudes in Jamaica have evolved somewhat since then, back in the 1970s, such a situation was deeply unsettling for someone like Burrel.

Unfortunately, Burrel's time at Concordia did not go as planned. Midway through the first semester, he began exhibiting troubling behavior and was hospitalized, where he was diagnosed with schizophrenia. Recognizing the severity of his condition, the university arranged for his return to Jamaica, accompanied by university personnel. It was heartbreaking to see him go, knowing how long we had been friends and how much he had hoped to achieve.

Back in Jamaica, Burrel moved in with his brother and was prescribed medication for his condition. Sadly, I later heard that he often refused to take his medication, which worsened his situation. Though I lost regular contact with him, the memory of his dreams and our shared history remains vivid. A reminder of how fragile and unpredictable life can be.

Malcolm had a highly successful first year at Concordia University, and during that time, we spent a lot of time together. We often hung out, including visits to the renowned strip club, Wanda, on Rue De Maisonneuve. At the time, Malcolm had left his young wife, Pam, and their baby back in Jamaica so that he could pursue his higher education. I could sense that the separation caused considerable stress for both. After completing his first year, Malcolm made the decision to return to Jamaica, where he enrolled at the University of the West Indies. There, he successfully completed his undergraduate degree in Business and later went on to pursue a master's degree in the same field.

His dedication and hard work paid off, and Malcolm went on to have a distinguished and prosperous career. Now in retirement, he enjoys the fruits of his labor. Despite the passage of time, we remain close friends and continue to stay in regular contact, sharing updates and reminiscing about the past.

CHAPTER 22

From Campus Leadership to Survival Hustles

In 1979, I was elected president of the Caribbean Student Association at the Loyola campus, an organization created to unite Caribbean students on campus and assist newcomers in adjusting to their new environment. Given the limited on-campus accommodation, one of our primary tasks was helping these students find nearby apartments. Many of them were 18 years old, leaving home for the first time and navigating the stress of moving to a foreign country. To ease their transition, we would often meet in one of the student lounges to socialize, share experiences, and discuss the latest news from the various Caribbean islands.

One of the highlights of the year was arranging a recording session just before Christmas. Students would send heartfelt Christmas greetings to their families back home in the Caribbean. This tradition had been going on for many years, where on Christmas Day, the radio stations broadcast Christmas messages from university students abroad to their loved ones back home.

Each student association was allocated a modest budget by the university to fund activities, and part of that budget went toward organizing social events, such as parties. These gatherings provided an excellent opportunity for Caribbean students to mingle and unwind. To ensure the parties went smoothly, I had to navigate the local bureaucracy to obtain a liquor license, and I would purchase alcohol on a consignment basis from the local liquor store, which allowed me to return any unsold inventory.

One memorable event was a party where we managed to hire a live band at a minimal cost. My friend, Byron Lee Jr., son of the famous Jamaican bandleader Byron Lee Sr., arranged for his father's band, Byron Lee and the Dragonaires, to perform. The band's music arranger and director, along with several other members of the group, played at the event, drawing a large crowd and delivering a fantastic performance that everyone thoroughly enjoyed.

In addition to our social activities, there was a larger Caribbean Student Association network. Each year, an inter-university Caribbean sports weekend was organized by the Caribbean Student Association at Sir George Williams Campus. Caribbean students from various universities in Quebec and Ontario participated in the event, fostering a strong sense of community among Caribbean students in the region.

On a more academic front, I became increasingly involved with the Computer Science Association, which was part of the Faculty of Engineering. The department was growing rapidly as more students enrolled in the program. To better serve the needs of this expanding student body, a group of us formed the Computer Science Student Association on the Loyola campus, where I was elected secretary.

In my final year, I also took on the roles of tutor and marker, helping first year students with their assignments and grading their work. These responsibilities were both rewarding and financially compensated, giving me the opportunity to further immerse myself in both the academic and social aspects of university life.

While my days were filled with academic commitments and campus leadership, life outside the university walls told a different story. Behind the student association meetings and tutoring sessions lay a constant struggle to make ends meet. With limited student loans and rising living costs, I had to get creative and resourceful to support Avril and myself. What followed was a humbling and eye-opening chapter, where survival meant taking on any honest work I could find, no matter how far it was from the dreams I carried when I first set foot on campus.

I was urgently in need of a job to cover my university expenses. My student loan from Jamaica was quite limited, so by the end of the first year, Avril's paycheck was covering both our living expenses and tuition fees. Unfortunately, she was working as a domestic helper, which didn't pay much.

I often conversed with a man in the apartment building where I lived on St. Jacques. I had assumed he was the building's owner because of the flashy car he drove, but to my surprise, he was the janitor. Coming from rural Jamaica, I wasn't familiar with the role of a janitor or their duties. I was curious, so one day I asked him about his responsibilities. He explained that as a janitor, he collected the rent, took out the garbage, cleaned the common areas, and kept the surroundings of the building tidy, all in exchange for free rent. I thought to myself, "That sounds like a great deal! It wouldn't take much of my time, and it could help with our expenses."

I decided to act and placed an ad in the Montreal Gazette reading: "University Student Looking for Part-Time Janitorial Work." Soon, I received a response from a large apartment management company, offering a janitorial position at one of their smaller buildings on Mountain Street in downtown Montreal. Avril and I went for the interview, and we both got the job. The building was a five-story structure with around 30 apartments.

The building was called Executive House, and it was located in an upscale area at the top of Mountain Street, just below Mount Royal Park. It was surrounded by prominent figures and landmarks, including former Prime Minister Pierre Trudeau's residence, Premier René Lévesque's condominium, the Cuban embassy, and several European embassies. I would occasionally run into René Lévesque himself at the convenience store below his condo, where he would stop by to pick up cigarettes. We even had a few casual conversations.

In my new role, I was responsible for collecting and disposing of the garbage from the rooms on each floor, vacuuming the hallways, mopping the lobby, and sometimes collecting rent cheques that were slipped under our door. In return for my janitorial duties, Avril and I received free rent for a 3.5-room apartment, which included two bedrooms, a living room, a kitchenette, and a bathroom. Additionally, we were given free cable TV.

To make extra money, I began collecting bottles from the garbage room and saving them. On our first wedding anniversary, I sold the bottles and earned $39. With that money, we were able to enjoy a special evening at a fancy restaurant on Mountain Street, where we had a full-course meal with drinks and desserts.

Despite my efforts to earn additional income, there was a significant obstacle. Back then, foreign students like me faced challenges in securing a job. Employers required a Social Insurance

Number (SIN), but since foreign students weren't permitted to work, our SINs wouldn't authorize us for employment in Canada. This created a dead end for me in my search for additional work.

While the janitorial job eased our financial burdens by covering rent, it wasn't enough. I needed cash in hand to help with daily expenses, books, and unexpected costs. But securing legal work was nearly impossible without a Social Insurance Number. Refusing to be defeated, I kept asking questions around campus, determined to find a way. That determination led me to a rougher, sweatier chapter of my life, one that tested my limits but also revealed the true meaning of survival.

I enquired around campus about finding a job without a SIN number, and I was told that some job agencies could help. These agencies allow you to register and find temporary, casual work, such as loading and unloading trucks at the wharf and various other locations.

During the summer break, I decided to visit one of these agencies and sign up. My first assignment was with a trucker who was picking up barrels of orange juice at the wharf. Those barrels were incredibly heavy, but I desperately needed the money. The following day, I went with another trucker to the wharf. This time, it was massive bags of flour. The intense summer heat caused my body to sweat profusely, and I found myself covered in a thick layer of flour paste.

I needed a break, so I took about 15 minutes to read the *Montreal Gazette*, which had become a routine of mine ever since I lived in Jamaica. I always made time to catch up on the news because I believed it was the best way to stay informed about the world.

However, the next day, when I returned to the agency, I was told I was fired. The truck driver had complained that I had been reading the newspaper during work hours. This left me feeling frustrated and disheartened. I reflected on my previous career as a high school teacher in Jamaica, where educators were highly respected in their communities, and here I was being let go from a menial, demeaning job.

I went home that day feeling discouraged, but after some thought, I decided to reinvent myself: I would become a house painter.

CHAPTER 23

From Grit to Belonging: Our Montreal Journey

After the embarrassment of being fired from a job I deemed utterly demeaning, I decided to take a bold step to turn things around. I placed an advertisement in the classified section of the Montreal Gazette with the simple yet confident headline: *"ALTI THE PAINTER - REASONABLE RATES, REFERENCES AVAILABLE."* Despite having no experience in painting, I convinced a few of my university friends, including Eddie Cousins, to provide me with glowing references. They were more than happy to help, even though I had never held a paintbrush in my life.

To my surprise, the phone began ringing with requests for painting jobs. One of the first calls was from a man who owned several rental properties. He needed someone to repaint an apartment for a new tenant who was about to move in. The apartment was a two-and-a-half, which in Montreal terms meant it was a one-bedroom with a living room, kitchen, and bathroom. The job seemed straightforward, so I eagerly accepted the offer and rushed to Pascal, a popular local hardware store at the time. It was my lucky day, as they had white paint on sale.

The problem was, I had no idea how much paint I would need, as I had never painted before. Still, I bought several cans, reasoning that I could always return for more if necessary. I began the job the very next day. By the second day, I had already run out of paint. When I went back to Pascal to replenish my supply, I discovered that the sale had ended, and the price of the paint had returned to its original, expensive rate. Not knowing much about painting, I opted for another brand of white paint that was cheaper, unaware that not all white paints are the same.

To help speed up the work, Avril would ride her bicycle after work to assist me with the painting. We worked hard to finish the job, and I eagerly awaited the moment the owner would come to pay me for my first painting job. When he walked into the apartment, however, he stopped, looked at the walls, and then looked at me in disbelief. "What the F@&# did you do to my apartment?" he exclaimed.

I was taken aback because I thought I had done a great job. The owner, an older Jewish gentleman, walked over to me, put a hand on my shoulder, and said, "Son, I don't think you've ever painted before, have you?" He explained that not all white paints are the same, they can vary in shades and tones, and that I would need to repaint the apartment using the exact shade of white paint.

Although I was forced to redo the entire job at a financial loss, the experience taught me a valuable lesson about the nuances of painting. Despite the setback, more painting jobs continued to come my way, and Avril and I worked tirelessly to complete them as quickly as possible.

As we gained experience, we became quite proficient at painting. I decided to approach the manager of the apartment building where Avril and I lived and worked as janitors. I suggested that I could save the company money by painting the apartments myself when tenants moved out instead of hiring expensive contractors. To my surprise, he agreed.

Soon, I was earning a substantial income, enough to save up and buy a plane ticket for my mother to visit us in Montreal. It felt incredibly rewarding to not only make money for my tuition but also to be able to share the success with my mother. Outside of painting jobs and university work, life in Montreal brought many new experiences, especially during the winter months. Although I was no fan of the cold, I discovered creative ways to enjoy the season and embraced both its challenges and small pleasures.

During my time in Montreal, I didn't particularly enjoy the winter months, mainly because I didn't engage in typical winter activities like ice skating or skiing. However, I did find a way to make the most of the cold season. While exploring the underground parking garage of my building, I discovered a wooden box, roughly 3 feet by 5 feet, and a couple of old skis lying around. I decided to get creative and nailed the skis to the bottom of the box. Afterward, I took it to the top of the steep hill on Mount Royal, where crowds of people were tobogganing. As I reached the summit, I would signal the crowd with a loud "all clear," and they would move aside to make way for me. My makeshift contraption was so heavy and fast that it shot down the hill like a bullet, speeding across the frozen lake before coming to a halt, only to be stopped by some concrete barriers. Eventually, I was politely asked not to return, as my wild ride was endangering other tobogganers in the area.

Another winter tradition I grew fond of was the Sugaring-Off Party. This was a fun outdoor event, often held around late winter or early spring, where a fire crackled in a pit while large troughs filled with snow were set up. Buckets of freshly made maple syrup were placed nearby, and participants would dip sticks, similar to Popsicle sticks, into the syrup before twirling them in the snow to create maple taffy. Once I'd had my fill of the sweet treat, I'd head to the bar for a couple of beers to complete the experience.

The summer months in Montreal, however, were fantastic. Avril and I both had bicycles, which made weekends a lot of fun as we would go on long rides together. One of our favourite routes was along the Lachine Canal, and we would often cross over the Concord Bridge to Saint Helen's Island, home of the iconic Expo 67, which had drawn over 50 million visitors. Mount Royal Park was within walking distance of our apartment, making it an ideal location for our weekend picnics. On Saturday nights, we would take a casual stroll down to St. Catherine Street, where the crowds were always bustling. The area was known for its lively nightlife, and traffic jams were a regular occurrence, as people lingered out on the streets until the early hours of the morning. Crescent Street was the hot spot, home to the popular Sir Winston Churchill bar, a well-known hangout spot that still thrives to this day.

As my university studies were ending, the time had come for Avril and I to seriously consider our future. We had to think about where we would live and how we would find jobs. Our ideal plan was to stay in Canada, as we had grown fond of the country. We had settled in well, embraced its culture, and felt at home there. However, there was a major hurdle: we were not able to stay legally. I only held a student visa, which did not allow me to work, and Avril had a domestic visa, so we were effectively at a standstill in our plans.

To resolve this, Avril reached out to her employers, Ann and Lawrence, to ask if they would be willing to sponsor us for residency in Canada. They graciously agreed, and we were soon contacted by the Canadian Immigration Office to attend an interview in New York. We were thrilled not only by the opportunity to have our case considered but also by the chance to visit New York, a city we had never been to before. We decided to take the overnight train and stayed with a cousin who lived there.

When we arrived in New York the next day, we made our way to the Canadian Immigration Office, eager to attend the interview. Unfortunately, the moment we arrived, a gentleman informed us that our application had been rejected. We tried to explain that we had been sponsored by Avril's employers and showed him the letter that confirmed our interview, but he was adamant that there was nothing he could do to help us.

As we stood there, disheartened and in disbelief, a Quebec Immigration Officer, who had overheard our conversation, stopped and spoke with us. Despite our initial disappointment, he invited us into his office to discuss the matter further. He asked me what degree I was graduating with, and when I told him it was in Computer Science and Mathematics, he responded, "It's graduates like you that we need in Quebec." He handed me his business card and told me to reach out to him once we returned to Montreal.

That encounter turned out to be one of the happiest moments of my life. We left his office filled with hope and optimism, knowing that things might just work out. A couple of days later, after we returned to Montreal, I called him as instructed. Within just a few months, we received our landed status in Canada.

It was later that I learned about the unique provision in the Constitution Act of 1867, which states that immigration is one of the few areas of governance shared between the provincial and federal governments. This allowed us to navigate a path that we might not have thought possible, and we were forever grateful for the chance to stay in the country we had grown to love.

CHAPTER 24

Fixing Car Engines, Starting a Family, and Camping Tales

As my university studies were ending and we found ourselves in our late twenties, the thought of starting a family began to take root. It was clear that if we were going to have children, we would need to secure reliable transportation for doctor's appointments and other essential errands. So, one day, I visited a used car dealership on Saint Jacques in Montreal West, where I stumbled upon a 1973 AMC Javelin that I instantly fell in love with. For just $700, I made the purchase, excited about the prospect of having a vehicle that would serve our future needs. However, my excitement was short-lived. Less than a week later, the car stopped running. The timing chain had failed, and I was certain the dealer who had sold it to me was aware of the problem. When I called him to ask for help, he refused to take responsibility.

The design of older cars like the Javelin meant that the timing chain was situated deep within the engine, requiring a significant amount of work just to access it. In this case, taking it to a

113

mechanic to fix the problem would cost more than the car itself, something we simply couldn't afford. Determined not to give up, I went out and purchased a Chilton Repair Manual specifically for the AMC Javelin. I devoured the manual day and night, learning everything I could before deciding to take on the daunting task of repairing the car myself. I reasoned that the worst-case scenario would be that I couldn't fix it, in which case, I would just have the car hauled away to the scrapyard.

With my apprentice Avril by my side, we went into the underground garage in our apartment building to embark on a mission of changing the timing chain in our AMC Javelin. The garage was mostly empty, as many people living in downtown Montreal relied on public transportation rather than owning a car. I began the meticulous process of dismantling the car, handing the parts to Avril, who carefully labeled and bagged them according to where they were removed from. I then used a rope to rig up a "come-along pulley" system, hooking it over a sewer pipe that ran across the garage ceiling, and hoisted the engine cylinder head out. Once I had clear access, I discovered the broken timing chain, which I carefully removed and took to an auto parts shop where they provided me with the correct replacement part.

The next day, Avril and I were back at it, reassembling the car and reinstalling the parts as we had taken them out. We followed the instructions in the repair manual to the letter, timing the engine carefully. Finally, the moment of truth arrived: would the car start, or would we need to have it towed away? Avril was the one to turn the key, and after a tense moment, the engine coughed. I urged her to try again, and this time, the car roared to life. We couldn't contain our joy as we jumped in celebration, proud of our hard-earned success. We had done it, and now we were officially mechanics. This experience marked the beginning of a new chapter, one that would lead me to purchase, repair, and sell old cars for a profit, as well as take on the ambitious project of building my own 1929 Mercedes-Benz SSK, which I will detail further in the pages to come. Our newfound confidence after fixing the Javelin wasn't just about cars, it extended into how we approached life. With graduation approaching, we were eager to start a family, feeling ready to embrace the next chapter of adulthood.

In 1980, Avril found out she was pregnant, and it marked the beginning of an important chapter in our lives. We had been discussing the idea of starting a family for some time, especially as I had just one more year left to complete my university studies. We were both in our late twenties and, eager to move forward, didn't want to wait any longer. Back then, young couples often started families much earlier than we did. It was quite common for people to marry in their early twenties and immediately begin having children. But by the time we were ready, my generation was beginning to see the importance of establishing careers first before diving into parenthood.

It didn't take long for Avril to become pregnant, and I'm pretty sure it happened on one of our weekend camping trips.

When my first son, Mark, was born, it was without a doubt the most exciting and joyful moment of my entire life. For some fathers, there is a special wish for their firstborn to be a boy, but for me, it did not matter at all. All I truly wanted was to begin building a family. The dream of having a child had been in my heart for years, and finally, that dream had come true.

I am quite sure many fathers feel the same sense of overwhelming anticipation and fulfillment that I did when their child arrived. It is as if you have been waiting for this moment your whole life. Becoming a parent brings with it an indescribable feeling of connection and responsibility, as if you have just brought a part of yourself into the world. The arrival of your child does not just change your daily routine; it transforms everything about you and your world in ways you never imagined. It is an experience that will stay with you forever.

After we had repaired our AMC Javelin, it gave us great freedom to explore. Camping was a new adventure for both of us, so we went to Canadian Tire, a hardware store, and bought a tent and two sleeping bags that were on sale, not fully realizing that this was not all the gear we would need. But even if we had known, we wouldn't have been able to afford it anyway, as money was tight.

Having grown up as a country boy in Jamaica, I was used to being resourceful and improvising. So, we made do with what we had. I created a makeshift fire pit where we cooked all our meals. As complete novices in the world of camping, we assumed that all we needed to do was set up our tent, crawl into our sleeping bags without any padding beneath them, and go to sleep. But we quickly learned how wrong we were after that first night. It was a disaster. Tree roots and rocks poking into our backs made sleep nearly impossible.

The next day, we visited the nearest store and got some cardboard boxes, which we placed under our sleeping bags to ease the discomfort. While this helped a bit, it still wasn't enough. We spoke to other campers to figure out what they were using for a cushion and discovered that most were using bubble sheets as a cushion beneath their sleeping bags. Eager to improve our experience, we went to a camping store the following day and bought a few of those sheets. As our camping adventures continued, we eventually upgraded to a thick foam mattress, which made all the difference.

Looking back, it was a period of learning and growth, and it was certainly a memorable introduction to the joys and challenges of camping. Parenthood didn't slow us down. If anything, it made us more adventurous. Camping became our favourite weekend ritual, and even with a newborn, we were determined to keep the tradition alive, creating countless funny and unforgettable moments.

Our love for camping was so strong that every weekend during the summer, we eagerly headed to New York State, Vermont, and Massachusetts to immerse ourselves in the great outdoors. We even introduced our firstborn, Mark, to camping when he was just six weeks old. One of the highlights was dipping him in the lake, a memory that still brings smiles. One summer, Avril's parents came to visit, and we decided to take them along on our camping adventure. However, a cold front unexpectedly moved in the night we arrived, and it was clear that Avril's parents were struggling to keep warm. Noticing their discomfort, I quickly filled a two-litre plastic Coke bottle with hot water and handed it to them, suggesting they place it in their sleeping bag for extra warmth. While it did the trick and kept them warm throughout the night, they decided that camping wasn't for them, and we packed up and headed home the next day.

One evening, early on in our camping days, Avril and I decided to explore the campground's woods. As we wandered deeper, I spotted an animal that I thought was a rabbit, and, fueled by excitement, I chased it as fast as a cheetah chasing its prey. Just as I was about to catch it, the animal turned and lifted its tail, releasing an awful stench that took me completely by surprise. The foul odour overwhelmed me, choking me as I struggled to breathe.

Upon returning to our campsite, the smell was so intense that it prompted an alert from fellow campers about a skunk in the area. I had never encountered a skunk before, as there are none in Jamaica, and so, mistaking it for a rabbit, I had instinctively chased after it.

The next morning, we went to the nearby laundromat to wash our clothes, but despite our best efforts, the smell remained stubbornly strong. The odour was so potent that it sent people fleeing from the laundromat, and it lingered for days, creating an unpleasant atmosphere. At the campsite, we were shunned by other campers, and eventually, the clothes had to be discarded. Even after multiple showers and dousing myself with Avril's perfume, I still smelled like a skunk. The scent persisted, and when I returned to work, my colleagues couldn't help but mention that I had a distinct, unmistakable skunk odour.

I later learned that some people recommend washing yourself in tomato juice to remove the smell of skunk spray, though I can't say for sure if it works. All I know is that I would never, under any circumstances, want to find myself in that situation again. I certainly have no intention of testing that tomato juice remedy.

CHAPTER 25

Computer Programming, Wrenches, and Auto Craftsmanship

After graduating from university, I landed my first job at Dominion Textile, one of the largest textile companies at the time, known for supplying clients all over the world. I was hired as a programmer in the company's Information Technology (IT) department, where I was introduced to the programming languages used at the company: ASSEMBLY and COBOL. These computer languages were hosted on the IBM 360 platform, which may seem antiquated to young programmers today. While languages like COBOL and FORTRAN may not be as widely used anymore, many of today's programmers are likely familiar with ASSEMBLER, as it is one of the closest languages to Machine Language, the native language of computers.

My first project was a significant one: the implementation of a new barcode system. At the time, barcode technology was still in its early stages but was on the verge of becoming a worldwide standard. It was exciting to work on something that would eventually revolutionise industries across the globe.

During my time at Dominion Textile, I not only gained invaluable work experience but also made lifelong friendships. Many of the people I met there are still close friends to this day. Despite earning a good salary, Avril and I decided to keep our janitorial job at the apartment at the top of Mountain Street in Montreal. We had been living there for over two years, and the position allowed us to save money. We had no interest in renting and were determined to buy a home. Thanks to our efforts in continuing the janitorial job, we managed to save more than enough for a down payment on our first house, which became a major milestone in our lives.

While I was still employed at Dominion Textile, our family grew with the birth of my second son, Christopher. At the time, we were still living in a modest two-bedroom apartment at the top of Mountain Street, where I worked as the building janitor. With two children and only one salary coming in, since Avril had to stay home and care for them, I realised I needed to find some way to supplement our income.

As I've mentioned before, after replacing the timing chain in our AMC Javelin, I began to see myself as a bona fide mechanic, gaining confidence in my abilities. When Mark was born, our financial situation was tight; we had just $175 in the bank. Determined to turn things around, I decided to put my mechanical skills to the test.

One day, while browsing the classified ads in the Montreal Gazette, I saw an intriguing listing: a 1973 Volkswagen Beetle for just $75. I knew it was a bargain, so I called my good friend, Eddie Cousins, who had a car he'd inherited from his grandfather. Eddie and I became close friends after meeting at university in 1978, and despite our different backgrounds, we bonded over shared experiences. Eddie's father, a Jamaican, had studied engineering at McGill University, where he met Eddie's Polish Canadian mother. Eddie remains one of my best friends to this day.

Though we knew the Beetle couldn't be driven, Eddie and I decided to go pick the car up. We drove to Point Claire, Montreal, with a rope to tow the car back to my apartment building's garage, where I worked as the janitor. The building, located in downtown Montreal, had few tenants with cars, so I used the available spaces to my advantage.

What we didn't realise was that the Beetle's braking system was completely non-functional. Nevertheless, we had to find a way to get the car, about 25 kilometres away, to my place. Despite the risk, we hooked the rope on both cars and made our way onto the 2&20 Highway toward Montreal, hoping to avoid too many stops. With the flashers on, we cautiously entered the slow lane. Every time we needed to stop, Eddie would anticipate it, and I would "brake" by sticking my foot through a hole in the Beetle's floor panel, using the pavement to slow it down, just like the Flintstones. It was a crazy situation, but we made it to my apartment safely.

Once we got to my apartment building, I set to work on restoring the $75 Beetle. Armed with a pop-rivet gun, sheet metal, fiberglass, and some auto body filler. Next, I tackled the engine and the braking system, both of which I successfully fixed. I also wanted to learn about painting cars, so I visited a DIY (do-it-yourself) paint shop in St. Henry, Montreal, where I observed and asked questions. A week later, I returned, rented the painting booth, and gave the Beetle a fresh coat of bright yellow paint. To complete the look, I added black racing stripes along the roof and body, giving it a "Herbie the Love Bug" vibe.

121

After taking the Beetle for a few test drives to ensure everything was working properly, I decided to sell it. I advertised the car and, to my delight, sold it for $1,900. My initial investment of $75, plus another $200 in repairs and materials, had resulted in an impressive return of over 86%. I remember walking into the bedroom, throwing the $1,900 across the bed, and proudly showing Avril, "Look at all this money!" This was the moment I realised I had the potential for a successful entrepreneurial venture.

Invigorated by the success of my first sale, I began buying, repairing, painting, and selling more cars from the garage at my apartment. I also started doing repairs for my colleagues, handling everything from engine work to bodywork and painting. At the office, I became known as the go-to guy for car repairs and advice, and I soon found myself fully immersed in this new entrepreneurial path. With every car I fixed and sold, my skills and confidence kept growing. But after a while, I started craving a bigger challenge. Something that wasn't just about repairing, but about creating something from scratch. That's when I stumbled across the idea of building my own car. Not just restoring, but constructing a dream vehicle with my own hands.

I had mastered the art of rebuilding car engines, performing bodywork, and painting them, and I was ready for a new challenge, something beyond just repairing and refinishing cars. I wanted to create something entirely on my own. That's when the idea of building my own car took root. Back in the 1980s, car kits were a popular trend, frequently advertised in car magazines, and there were plenty of options to choose from.

Among all the kits available, one that truly caught my attention was a 1929 Mercedes-Benz SSK replica, known as the "Gazelle," produced by Classic Motor Carriages, a company based in Florida (though I'm not sure if they're still around today). This kit was designed to be assembled on a Volkswagen Beetle or Ford Mustang chassis. I chose the Beetle chassis, specifically the 1973 model, as I was very familiar with the Volkswagen Beetles; I had restored and sold several over the years. In fact, I still have a few Beetle engines stashed in my garage, always telling myself that one day I'll get around to rebuilding them. But, of course, it hasn't happened yet.

By then, I had saved up quite a bit of money from repairing and selling cars out of my apartment building's garage, so I had enough funds to purchase the kit from Classic Motor Carriages. In 1983, I placed the order for the kit, which cost $10,000, a significant sum at the time. In today's money, that would be equivalent to over $31,000. The challenge, however, was getting the kit to Montreal at a reasonable cost. The kit was crated into several large boxes, and I needed to figure out the most affordable shipping method. After some research, I found a trucker who regularly drove an eighteen-wheeler between Florida and Montreal, transporting oranges. He agreed to transport my kit car snuggled between the loads of oranges, which would allow me to avoid paying for any customs duties. Unfortunately, that plan didn't go as smoothly as I had hoped.

While I was at work one day, I received a call from the truck driver at the Canadian and US border. Customs had randomly inspected his truck and discovered the kit car boxes. As a result, I had to go to the border to settle the customs duties before they released the truck. I went down, paid the fees, and finally, both the truckload of oranges and my kit car were cleared for delivery. My friend Colin Barrens, whom I had introduced to Pat Ferretti at Dominion Textile, came to help me unload the boxes from the truck and into the garage of my apartment building.

At that point, I had already bought the 1973 Volkswagen Beetle that I would use as the base for my kit car. It was in excellent condition, both the engine and the body, and I was eager to start the build.

CHAPTER 26

Building the Car and the Blueprints for a Better Life

The kit car arrived with a detailed manual outlining the steps required to prepare the Beetle chassis for the new kit car. Eager to get started, I rolled up my sleeves and set to work, removing the seats and various parts. Once I had stripped the chassis down, I began loosening the nuts and bolts that secured the body to the frame.

Next came the task of lifting the body off the chassis. When Avril put the kids to bed, she joined me in the garage, which was conveniently located just down the hallway from our apartment on the ground floor. Together, we carefully hooked ropes to the Beetle's body and secured another rope around a sturdy six-inch cast iron sewer pipe above. Using my "come-along pulleys," we ratcheted the body off the chassis with precision.

With the body removed, I turned my attention to the chassis itself. I needed to make some modifications to ensure it would fit the kit car. This involved moving the entire pedal cluster about six to eight inches back, a task that required cutting and welding the chassis to accommodate the new configuration.

The Beetle chassis I was working on was surprisingly in very good condition, with very little rust, an uncommon find in Montreal. Next, I searched for a Beetle with a solid chassis base but a rusted upper body. It didn't take long to find one, and I quickly brought it back to my apartment garage. There, I repeated the same process I had used for the kit car base: stripping it down and transferring the good body from the kit car chassis onto my new purchase. After giving it a fresh coat of paint, I sold the rusted upper body to the scrapyard, and the complete car fetched far more than I had initially paid for both Beetles. Simply put I bought two Beetles, the one I used for my kit car had very good upper so I switched it with the 2nd Beetle that had a rusted upper body.

With the Beetles cleared out of my garage, I was ready to focus on my dream project: building a 1929 Mercedes-Benz SSK. After work and on weekends, I dedicated myself to the building. Supper was often already prepared when I returned home, giving me time to enjoy moments with Avril and the kids. Occasionally, they would come into the garage to watch me work, and on weekends, two-year-old Mark would be my little assistant, giving Avril a much-needed break.

The most difficult part of the building was wiring. The manual suggested using the same wire color-coding scheme as the Volkswagen Beetle, as well as the relays and fuse clusters. I picked up a Chilton Volkswagen Manual that included the necessary wiring diagrams and set to work.

In just over three months, I completed the project. The car had to pass a thorough inspection by the Quebec Transportation Engineers and the Quebec Motor Vehicle Registration Bureau. I conducted extensive checks myself, testing the electrical systems, mechanical components, heating, and overall performance. To ensure everything was in perfect working order, I took it to a parking lot and pushed it through rigorous driving and maneuvering tests.

Since the car was considered new, unregistered, it required certification that it wasn't stolen. I took it to the Montreal Police Headquarters for this purpose and then made an appointment with the Quebec Ministry of Transportation for further inspections by their engineers. Finally, I visited the Quebec Motor Vehicle Registration Bureau to obtain a serial number and license plate. I even splurged on a personalized plate: "ALTY." After passing all the tests with flying colors, I waited at the Bureau while the examiners took turns enjoying a joyride in the car.

I still have the Mercedes-Benz SSK parked in my garage, though it has been a while since I've driven it. My grown sons still call it the "Baby Car," a nickname they've used since childhood. Completing the Mercedes-Benz SSK was more than just finishing a car; it felt like I had crossed a personal milestone. But as I looked around at our growing family and changing circumstances, I realized it was time to focus on building something even more important. A stable, comfortable home for us all. That's when I set my sights on advancing my professional career and securing a proper house where we could put down deeper roots.

In the early 1980s, the demand for computer programmers was soaring, making it a prime time for career advancement in the tech industry. To secure higher salaries and better opportunities, professionals often moved between companies. I decided to apply for a position as a Senior Programmer at Canadair, a well-known company located in Ville Saint Laurent, Montreal. Canadair was later acquired by Bombardier and eventually merged with the

Toronto-based De Havilland Aircraft, expanding its reach in the aviation industry.

By making this career move, I received a significant salary increase, which prompted us to reevaluate our situation. After careful consideration, we decided it was time to leave our janitorial jobs. Positions that had served us well and provided invaluable experience, but now we could afford something better.

Keeping the janitorial job while I was working allowed us to save quite a large sum of money from my job, and with my new salary boost, we began the exciting process of house hunting. Our search was focused on the West Island, an area conveniently located near my new workplace at Canadair. After viewing several homes, we found an older four-bedroom detached bungalow in Pierrefonds, priced at $42,000. This house, nestled in a neighbourhood with large, mature trees, offered both charm and potential. The huge front and back yards were perfect for our needs. In the back of my mind, I imagined building a large garage while still retaining plenty of space for outdoor activities. It felt like the ideal place to start the next chapter of our lives.

Several residents of my new neighbourhood in Pierrefonds worked at Canadair, as it was conveniently located nearby. One of my next-door neighbours, Hank, was an older gentleman originally from Holland. He had an impressive background as a flight engineer with KLM Airlines before being hired by Canadair as an aeronautical engineer. Hank shared with me that he was the lead engineer behind the braking system design for the Challenger Executive jets, which continue to be in use to this day.

Another neighbour, Desmond Kack, worked in the accounting department at Canadair. He suggested we carpool to work, and we took turns driving. This arrangement allowed our wives to have a vehicle available for errands, doctor's appointments, and taking care of the kids.

I recall a funny but somewhat scary incident one morning during one of our carpool rides. I was driving my 1973 Mercedes-Benz when it suddenly stalled at a stoplight and refused to start. While Desmond remained in the passenger seat, I opened the hood to try and figure out the issue. In my haste, I started the car from the engine compartment without realizing I had failed to put the car in park. To my surprise, the car lurched forward with me still leaning over the engine. In a split second, Desmond acted quickly, slamming on the brakes, which sent me tumbling to the ground. Despite the scare, we couldn't help but laugh at the absurdity of the situation, and after a brief moment, we were on our way to work.

Pierrefonds was a wonderful neighbourhood, complete with a community swimming pool, soccer fields, baseball diamonds, and an outdoor ice rink. It was also conveniently located within walking distance of several restaurants and the well-known Fairview Mall. The residents were all incredibly friendly and always willing to lend a hand whenever needed.

It didn't take long for me to become the go-to person in the neighbourhood for car troubles. One of my neighbours, an avid camper who had recently upgraded to a new trailer, came to me with car issues. After I fixed his car, he offered me his old soft-top trailer as payment. The trailer, which could sleep six people, was a fantastic gift. At the time, my family and I were still using tents for camping, so this new trailer made our camping trips much more comfortable and enjoyable.

CHAPTER 27

Our New Neighbourhood

After transitioning to my new job at Canadair, I not only gained new clients for car repairs but also continued to work with people from my previous employer, Dominion Textile. With the growing demand for my services, I found myself working out of an open carport, which quickly became inadequate. Recognizing the space available to me, I decided to build a proper garage. I took the time to design detailed plans and submitted them to the City of Pierrefonds for approval. Once my permit was granted, it was time to get started.

I began the excavation process, with the "help" of my two young boys, Mark, two and a half years old, and Chris, just a year and a half old. Despite their small size, they were eager to join in, even if their contribution was more of a distraction than actual assistance! This project quickly became a neighbourhood spectacle. In our area, no one had ever built a freestanding garage before, so the men in the neighbourhood took a keen interest in my endeavor.

When I reached the framing stage, the local "handyman" crew, eager to contribute their skills or simply to observe, showed up in full force. Their excitement was contagious, and I even had Avril waking me up on weekends, telling me that the guys were out there ready to help. The camaraderie was uplifting; Avril and I quickly became part of the social fabric of the neighbourhood, with Avril connecting with the wives, as the area was filled with young families.

Life with our growing family was incredibly rewarding. Between my stable job at Canadair and the side income from my car repair business, we were financially comfortable. Living on a single salary made it possible for Avril to stay at home with the kids, which was a source of happiness for both of us. When I came home from work in the evenings, I would take the boys to the park or go on bike rides around the neighbourhood. We also created a new family tradition: on Saturdays, Avril would take the night off from cooking, and we would eat out at a restaurant. This tradition continues to this day.

Avril had always wanted a girl, but after our two boys, I was hoping for a larger family, as I grew up with four siblings. Despite our differing wishes, Avril became pregnant again, hoping this time it would be the daughter she longed for. However, fate had other plans, and on November 11, 1984, we welcomed our third son, Ian.

We called on our next-door neighbour, Barbara, who had kindly offered to help whenever the baby arrived. I drove Avril to the hospital and assisted with the delivery, just as I had with Mark and Chris. Afterward, I went home to gather the boys and brought them to the hospital to meet their new brother. As we were getting ready to leave, I realized that Mark was missing. After a quick search, we found him hiding under the bed where Avril had just given birth. He didn't want to leave his mommy.

Avril stayed in the hospital for a few days, and when she finally came home, the two boys and I had made a large banner that we hung across the living room to welcome her and Ian back. It was a heartfelt moment for our growing family, one that symbolized the joy and love we shared as we embarked on this next chapter of our lives.

I had become quite comfortable at Canadair, my new workplace, where I had formed many new friendships. One of my favorite parts of the day was walking through the airplane assembly plant during my lunch break, marveling at the intricate process of how the aircraft were built. The company placed great importance on fostering a positive and enjoyable atmosphere for its employees, which was evident in the numerous social activities it organized.

Every Christmas, the company threw a festive party for all employees and their families. It was a heartwarming event where children had the chance to meet Santa Claus, receive gifts, and even get their faces painted. In addition to this, there were various organized sports teams, including soccer and softball, among others. Given the large number of company employees, there were multiple teams in each sport, creating a competitive and lively atmosphere.

Having grown up in Jamaica, I was familiar with playing soccer/football and cricket. However, I wanted to try something new and decided to join the IT department's softball team. Back in Jamaica, we played a game similar to softball called "Base," where instead of using a bat, we hit a tennis ball with our bare hands after it was tossed underhand. While some of the rules in softball were reminiscent of our game "Base," they were quite different from cricket.

In cricket, if the ball is caught in the infield, the area within the boundaries of the field, the batter is out, and the play stops until a new batter takes his/her place. In contrast, softball allows the play to continue even if the ball is caught in the infield, and a runner can advance, potentially scoring a run. This means that the ball must be returned to the infield as quickly as possible to prevent the other team from scoring.

At my first baseball game, I was assigned the position of center fielder, largely because the coaches had seen how far and accurately I could throw the ball, a skill I had developed from playing cricket. I took my place in the outfield, but without a glove, since I had never used one before. In cricket, players in the outfield don't wear gloves; only the wicketkeeper does.

During one game, the opposing team's star hitter stepped up to the plate with runners on first and second base. He launched the ball deep into the center field, right where I was stationed. I sprinted after it, tracking the ball with the precision of a gazelle, and made a diving catch, bare-handed as I would have done in a cricket match. The crowd erupted in cheers, and I decided to add a dramatic flair to the play, as I would have done in cricket. I rolled over, jumped to my feet, and tossed the ball in the air, catching it again in a move we call "styling" or "hotdogging" in cricket. Everyone on the field was shouting at me excitedly to throw the ball in, and I assumed they were all still applauding my incredible catch. However, my joy was short-lived when the right fielder grabbed the ball from me and threw it in, but not before the go-ahead run crossed the plate.

I could see the disappointment on my teammates' faces. The energy shifted from celebration to frustration, and I knew I had made a costly mistake. The game was now in the bottom of the ninth inning, and with two runners on first and second and two outs, we were trailing by a run. It was my turn to bat. Since I was inexperienced, I was positioned at the bottom of the lineup. As I stepped up to the plate, I instinctively placed my bat on the ground, as I had done in cricket. The opposing team immediately began chanting, "Cricketer! Cricketer!" while my teammates shouted at me to hold the bat upright, which was foreign to me. I tried to adjust, but nothing felt right. So, I returned to my cricket stance, with the bat resting on the home plate.

Back when I played cricket, I had earned the nickname "wild hitter" from my brothers. I wasn't known for hitting elegant or refined shots; rather, I was the type to swing for the fences and hit the ball out of the ground for six runs. My brothers, Valin and Leslie, were accomplished cricketers who played County cricket in Jamaica and had a large following of fans.

Now, it was a make-or-break moment. I stood there with my bat on the ground, the tension thick in the air. My teammates were holding their breath, while the opposing team continued their chant, "Cricketer! Cricketer!" The pitcher wound up and threw a low pitch right in my wheelhouse. I swung with excitement, and the bat made perfect contact with the ball, sending it soaring like a rocket into the parking lot. The crowd went wild, and the team erupted in jubilation. I had delivered for the team.

From that moment on, I became known as their number one slugger, and my wild cricket swings had earned their place in Canadair baseball stories. Life in Pierrefonds was full of warmth, community, and personal milestones. But as the boys began to grow and we looked toward their future, the landscape around us was also shifting. New language laws were changing the way families like ours navigated life in Quebec, and career opportunities were calling from beyond provincial borders. What began as a simple life in a tight-knit neighbourhood was about to pivot into something bigger, one spontaneous decision at a time.

When my eldest son, Mark, began attending a bilingual day-care in our neighbourhood, we thought it would be a great opportunity for him to learn French. After all, we were living in Montreal, where French is predominantly spoken. In the West Island, where we resided, cities like Pierrefonds, Dollard-des-Ormeaux, Dorval, Pointe-Claire, and others were primarily English-speaking, and French was not commonly heard. In fact, at that time, the primary office language in Montreal was English.

However, everything changed when Bill 101, the language law, was enacted. One of its key provisions was that children whose parents did not have their primary education in French would be required to attend French-language schools. This new rule applied to us, as my education in Montreal had been at the university level, and I had not attended primary or high school in Quebec.

As Avril and I thought more seriously about this law, we became increasingly concerned about how we would support our children with their homework, as we weren't fluent enough in French to guide them effectively. Additionally, Bill 101 stipulated that French would be the language of business in the province, meaning English would no longer be the default in many workplaces.

We started to seriously consider relocating to Ontario, and we weren't the only ones facing these challenges. Hundreds of companies and thousands of people were making the same decision, seeking an environment where their children could have access to an education in both languages and where business was conducted primarily in English.

From my perspective, Bill 101 didn't serve the French-speaking population as much as it was intended to. In fact, I believe English-speaking immigrants were better positioned under the new law. Here's why: while French-speaking children were required to attend French schools, English-speaking immigrant children, whose parents had not completed their primary education in English in the Province of Quebec, were also placed in French schools.

However, while French-speaking children spoke French at home, the children of English-speaking immigrants often spoke English at home, which meant they naturally became bilingual. This linguistic advantage made them more appealing to employers, as most companies in Montreal preferred hiring bilingual individuals. The result was that, in some ways, the law inadvertently favored English-speaking immigrants while placing a significant burden on the French-speaking population. Amidst these growing concerns about our children's future and the shifting professional landscape, Avril and I found ourselves increasingly restless. We had always been open to change and adventure, and with every conversation about the limitations we faced in Quebec, the idea of exploring new possibilities became more appealing. It wasn't long before that restlessness sparked an idea that would soon take us on an unexpected journey.

CHAPTER 28

Highway 401: Journey to a New Life in Ontario

Avril and I have always been spontaneous, rarely overthinking our decisions. So, on Boxing Day in 1985, while we sat around the dining table in the kitchen with the kids, I turned to Avril and suggested, "Why don't we drive to Toronto tomorrow?" Toronto, 600 kilometers away from Montreal, seemed like an ambitious idea, but I was feeling bold. "We can stay with my Aunt Pearl, drive around, explore job opportunities, and see if we like the city." Avril agreed without hesitation, as that's how we approached most things, impulsively.

I quickly picked up the phone to call Aunt Pearl and let her know that we would be visiting the next day. Some readers might find it rude to show up with such short notice to my aunt, but for us, it is a Jamaican thing we do. Aunt Pearl was genuinely delighted to hear from us and was excited about the visit.

The following day, we packed the car with all three boys and set off for Toronto. It was a pleasant drive, and when we arrived, it was wonderful to reconnect with Aunt Pearl and her family. We got together with my cousin Ray, who had been our host when we first arrived in Canada, and we also spent time with Stanford, Janet, and Evette, my other cousins.

While in Toronto, I thought about Danny Nissenbaum, a former colleague from my Canadair days, who had moved there a year earlier to work at McDonnell Douglas. Danny had mentioned that the company was looking for IT personnel, so I decided to check it out. Aunt Pearl lived in Scarborough, which is on the east side of Toronto, while McDonnell Douglas was located across the city in the west end, near Pearson International Airport.

Avril, the boys, and I drove across Toronto to McDonnell Douglas. I went into the building to speak with someone from the HR department about job opportunities, while Avril and the boys waited in the car, watching the planes taking off and landing at the airport, which shared a fence with the company. The sound of the planes and the excitement of being in a new place added to the sense of adventure.

When I returned to the car, I was thrilled. The HR representative had informed me that McDonnell Douglas was indeed hiring and would be happy to bring me on board. I was optimistic that my experience working at another aircraft company would make the transition a smooth one. It was an exciting moment for us, filled with hope and the promise of new opportunities.

A few days after returning to Montreal, I updated my resume and sent it to the HR department at McDonnell Douglas. To my surprise, the following week I received a call from an IT consulting company that informed me they were interested in flying me to Toronto for an interview with McDonnell Douglas. I agreed, and soon after, I received a plane ticket. The next week, I found myself at McDonnell Douglas for the interview. The consulting company, independent of McDonnell Douglas, was responsible for supplying IT personnel to the company. They offered me a starting salary of $40,000, a figure that felt like a dream come true. At the time, earning $40,000 was considered a solid benchmark for financial success.

I had the entire day to spend in Toronto, as my return flight to Montreal wasn't until later that evening. I took a shuttle bus into the city, enjoyed a leisurely lunch, strolled around, and then made my way back to the airport for my flight home. Everything was moving at such a fast pace that it was hard to keep up. When I got back to Montreal, Avril and I sat down to discuss our next steps, as the company wanted me to start at the beginning of February. With less than three weeks left in January, we had a lot to organize. Our house needed to be sold, I had to give notice at my current job, and we had to figure out how Avril would manage with our three young boys while being apart from me.

After discussing it thoroughly, we decided to go for it. I handed in my two weeks' notice at work, which shocked everyone, and we decided to list our house privately to avoid paying a real estate commission fee. To our surprise, the house sold quickly and will be closing by the end of April. Now, we needed to find a place to live in Toronto. The challenge was that we had no idea where the best neighbourhoods were, so we contacted a realtor. We explained that we were driving from Montreal and were looking for a house within reasonable proximity to McDonnell Douglas.

The next week, Avril, the boys, and I drove back to Toronto, optimistic that we would find a beautiful, spacious home like the one we had just sold in Montreal, which had yielded a $25,000 profit over three years. However, our excitement quickly turned to disappointment when we met our realtor in Mississauga and saw the steep prices of homes there. It was 1986, and the housing market was on the rise. We realized that buying a home in Mississauga was out of our budget, so we asked the realtor if there were any more affordable areas nearby. She suggested Burlington, a city located a bit further from McDonnell Douglas, where we might be able to find a house within our price range in the older part of the city. She referred us to another realtor in Burlington, and after meeting with her, we found a house we liked and made an offer.

We wanted to check how long the drive would be from Burlington to McDonnell Douglas, as I was considering commuting to work from there. As we made our way back to McDonnell Douglas, we saw an exit for a city called Brampton. Curiosity led us to take a brief detour into Brampton, driving around to get a feel for the area. We found ourselves quite drawn to the neighbourhood but were unsure about the prices of the local housing market.

To learn more, we stopped at a for-sale sign and jotted down the contact information of a realtor. After calling, the realtor seemed hesitant, initially suggesting we schedule an appointment for later in the week. However, when I mentioned that we were from Montreal and needed to purchase a home within the next two days, her attitude shifted dramatically. She quickly agreed to meet us within half an hour.

The homes we viewed in Brampton were noticeably more spacious and affordable compared to what we had seen in Mississauga and Burlington. We quickly decided to make an offer on a four-bedroom, multi-level semi-detached house priced at $93,000. Before finalizing anything, I made a call to the realtor in Burlington to formally withdraw our offer there. With the house secured, we drove back to Montreal feeling excited and proud of our successful home purchase.

Upon returning home, my office had organized a lunch at a local restaurant to celebrate my new chapter. It was at that dinner, surrounded by friends and colleagues, that it truly hit me. I was leaving Montreal, my second home, which I had grown to love deeply. Over the ten years I spent there, I had built strong relationships and cherished the vibrant community. The thought of leaving behind friends and familiar places brought tears to my eyes as I realized how much I would miss them all.

The original plan was for Avril to stay behind with our boys while I moved to Toronto alone. I was going to stay with Aunt Pearl until May, returning to Montreal not on a regular basis because of the 600-kilometer distance. Saying goodbye that day was heart-wrenching. Packing my beloved 1973 black Mercedes-Benz with a few personal belongings, hugging Avril and the boys tightly, and hearing the boys plead, "Dad, don't go." It broke my heart, as Avril and I had never been apart for ten years. Tears streaming down my face, I drove away towards Highway 2&20, heading east to connect with Highway 401 towards Toronto.

CHAPTER 29

Across Cities, To Toronto and Hopes

I arrived in Toronto to begin my new job at McDonnell Douglas. It was around eight in the evening when I reached Aunt Pearl's house, and she had dinner all ready for me. We shared a meal together, along with her youngest daughter, Evette, who was still living at home. After dinner, we chatted for a while before I retired to my room to unpack. I needed to rest, as I would have to be up early for work the next day.

McDonnell Douglas was located near Pearson International Airport, on the west end of Toronto. The commute would take over an hour, as I would have to travel across the city on the busy Highway 401. I tried to prepare myself for the long, high-traffic drive ahead.

That night, I had a restless sleep. My thoughts kept drifting back to Avril and the boys in Montreal. The reality of starting a new job made me anxious, and I couldn't help but feel the distance between me and my family. When you start a new job in IT, you're usually given manuals to read so you can familiarise yourself with the company's systems. McDonnell Douglas used a different database than Canadair. At Canadair, I worked with the TOTAL database, but at McDonnell Douglas, they used ADABAS. However, the software tools to access both databases were CICS and COBOL, which I had been using for years.

I did know one person at McDonnell Douglas, Danny, from the IT department. We worked together at Canadair. Danny showed me around the office, introduced me to other co-workers, and took me to the cafeteria, where lunch was offered at a reasonable price. The parking lot at McDonnell Douglas shared a fence with Pearson International Airport's runway, so during my lunch breaks, I would stand by the fence, watching planes land and take off.

My first week on the job was slow; I spent most of my time reading manuals and getting acquainted with my new environment. My mind kept wandering back to Montreal, thinking of Avril and the boys. I also realised I wouldn't be seeing them for a whole month, which was a very long time to be away from them.

When Friday came, marking the end of my first week, I headed back to Aunt Pearl's house, driving down Highway 401. But as I approached the exit to her place, I made an unexpected decision. I just kept driving. I was driving my black 1973 Mercedes-Benz 280 SE, and I couldn't stop thinking about how much I missed my family. Without any way to contact Avril, I just continued toward Montreal. I arrived at her door at around midnight, and when she opened it, she was taken aback to see me standing there. She asked what I was doing there, and I simply said, "The car just kept driving towards Montreal."

The next morning, the boys were thrilled to have me back home, and we spent an incredible weekend together. On Sunday evening, I drove back to Toronto, and that became my routine for the next five weeks: I would drive to Montreal every Friday evening and return to Toronto on Sunday night.

Although I was missing my family terribly, I made the best of the situation. After work each day, I would return to Aunt Pearl's house, where she had already prepared dinner. We had agreed that I would pay her for room and board for the five weeks I would be staying there, which worked out perfectly. After dinner, I would call Avril, chat with the boys, and when they went to bed, Avril and I would spend hours talking. It was a bittersweet time, balancing work, family, and the longing to be with them every day.

Though those five weeks of weekend commuting were exhausting, they gave me just enough strength to hold on until our family could finally reunite. The longing to be together again only made the moment sweeter when the time came to move everyone to Toronto.

The time had come for my family to relocate to Toronto, and the weekend before our big move, we had an incredible farewell party. It was a great party, as I had invited people I worked with at my different workplaces, Dominion Textile and Canadair, my neighbours, and other friends I had made while living in Montreal for ten years. The party was full of warmth and goodwill, and I truly appreciated their kindness.

In preparation for the move, I took a few days off from work. I left my car at Aunt Pearl's house and took the Voyager bus back to Montreal, as Avril would be driving the large Ford LTD to Toronto. We had rented an enormous 28-foot truck for the move, and my neighbours generously offered their help to pack it with all our belongings. Among the items we packed were two Volkswagen engines and several car parts from Mercedes-Benz and Volvo. There were a few things we couldn't fit, so we gave them away to our neighbours, who were grateful to receive them.

That Saturday, the day we left, was filled with bittersweet emotions. Saying goodbye to our neighbours was hard. Avril climbed into the Ford LTD with Chris and Ian, while Mark was excited to ride with me in the truck. As we drove away, we looked back, our hearts heavy, and saw our neighbours waving us off in the rear-view mirror. It was a sad yet hopeful moment for all of us.

We had bought a new house in Brampton, a suburb located northwest of Toronto. At the time, the population of Brampton was 195,920 and currently it is close to 800,000 according to the latest Canadian census. The closing of the sales agreement was scheduled for Monday, so I parked the truck on the street at Aunt Pearl's house for the weekend. On Monday, I drove it to work and parked it in the McDonnell Douglas lot. By the time the workday ended, the house was officially ours. I had made prior arrangements with my friends Danny and Jim, an American from Virginia, whom I had met at McDonnell Douglas. Danny, who had previously helped me move from my apartment in Montreal to Pierrefonds, was there to assist with this move as well.

Though the move was a bit hectic, everything came together in the end, and we were finally settled into our own home. The commute to McDonnell Douglas was smooth, taking only about twenty minutes each way, which made life much easier. I was earning enough that Avril didn't need to work, which was a relief. It allowed her to spend quality time with the boys, and she even volunteered at their school, which was a wonderful way for her to stay involved.

As we settled into our new life in Brampton, my natural instincts to plan ahead and seek financial growth began to resurface.

I couldn't help but look beyond the present comfort, wondering what more we could do to secure an even better future.

As you may have noticed, I am the kind of person who is always on the lookout for the next opportunity to improve my financial situation. In Jamaica, we have a term for this kind of drive and ambition; it's called "hustling." I took it upon myself to research the rental market in Brampton, and to my surprise, I discovered that the prices were far higher than I had anticipated. This led me to a realisation: renting in Brampton was far more expensive than we had expected, and it made me consider a new approach.

After careful thought, I convinced Avril that we should explore the option of renting out our house in Brampton and purchasing another property in Orangeville, a city situated to the north of Brampton, about a 40-minute drive from work. The property prices in Orangeville were significantly lower, which made it an attractive option. We started searching for homes there and eventually found a beautiful three-bedroom house, which was priced much lower than our Brampton home.

With our decision made, we approached Canada Trust, a financial institution at the time (which later merged with TD to form TD Canada Trust), to inquire about securing a mortgage for the new property. After reviewing our situation, they agreed to offer us the mortgage we needed to purchase the Orangeville house. We placed an offer on the house, and it was accepted. We were thrilled, and the closing date was set.

In the summer, we travelled to England to visit Avril's parents, and upon our return, we were eager to finalise everything and close on our new home. However, when we contacted our realtor to discuss the closing process, we were shocked to learn that Canada Trust had suddenly reversed its decision to offer us the mortgage. They provided no explanation for this unexpected change.

I was incredibly disappointed by this news, as it felt like a major setback. But I refused to let this disappointment derail my financial goals. Despite the setback, I remained determined to find another way to achieve my aspirations and not allow this one obstacle to define my journey.

Chapter 30

Roots and Growth in Brampton

After finishing university and beginning my career, I was in a stable financial position, which allowed me to fulfil an important family responsibility. In Jamaica, there's an unwritten cultural expectation that if a close relative migrates to a foreign country, they should help others from their family have the same opportunity. I decided to sponsor my parents to move to Canada. I submitted the application, and soon after, it was approved. In 1987, a year after we moved from Montreal to Toronto, my parents and my sister Colleen, along with her son Damion, arrived and lived with us for approximately six months. During this time, they found employment, which allowed them to rent an apartment of their own. However, other siblings remained in Jamaica, including my sister Sherron and her three children, Odette, Cassandra, and Kishawn, as well as my brother Leslie and his children, Kim and Javier. My brother Valin had migrated to the United States years before.

By then, my mother had become established in Canada, so we decided to sponsor the rest of the family to join us. With the anticipation of their arrival, I made the decision to buy another house in Brampton to accommodate them. I purchased a three-bedroom backsplit house and took the extra step of converting the basement into two additional bedrooms to ensure there would be enough space for them all.

As things settled at home, my professional life took an unexpected turn. What started as a promising opportunity through a consulting firm soon led me into the next big shift in my career.

While working at McDonnell Douglas, I was employed by a consulting firm called Data-Star, which was owned by two partners. Over time, tensions between the partners seemed to escalate, and I suspect this conflict led McDonnell Douglas to terminate all its contracts with the company. As a result, the employees, including myself, were given about a month to secure new positions.

During this period, one of the partners reached out to me. He invited me to join him on his yacht for a sail on Lake Ontario, where he proposed placing me at another company. Despite the opportunity, I decided to decline his offer, preferring instead to look for a new job on my own. Given the demand for my skills in the field, finding a new position wasn't particularly challenging.

I eventually landed a job at McKenzie Financial, a firm specialising in mutual funds, which was located on Bloor Street and Avenue Road, directly across from the Royal Ontario Museum in Toronto. Working there marked my first real exposure to the world of finance and provided me with valuable insights into how the industry operated.

Interestingly, about four years prior to my joining the company, a young Jamaican entrepreneur named Michael Lee-Chin had recognised the potential in McKenzie's mutual funds. At the time, he was selling their products, but his entrepreneurial spirit led him to see an opportunity for greater wealth. He borrowed $500,000 from the bank and used it to purchase a stake in McKenzie, ultimately making millions and laying the foundation for his financial empire. Although I didn't fully appreciate the potential of investing in mutual funds back then, when Lee-Chin later launched his own AIC Mutual Funds, I was ready. I decided to invest, and this decision would prove significant, as I'll detail later in the book.

As an IT consultant, my income was substantial, which allowed me to live a comfortable lifestyle. I was able to afford a larger home, drive nice cars, and take my family on vacation, enjoying the fruits of my hard work.

While work kept me busy, the real joy of life in Brampton came from family time. As the boys grew, sports, especially baseball, became a central part of our routine and brought us closer as a family and community.

When my eldest son Mark turned six, I found myself diving into the world of coaching baseball. Both Avril and I had been active in sports throughout our lives. Avril had a strong background in netball and tennis and had even earned the title of Junior Champion for the City of York, England. As for me, I had earned the title of Athlete Champion Boy/Athlete of the Year for my school, and I had also played cricket, the world's second most popular sport, just behind football (soccer). It always amuses me when North Americans refer to baseball, American football, hockey, and basketball as "World Champions," considering these sports are mostly played in North America.

We decided to enroll Mark in a house league baseball program, which was hugely popular in Brampton and across Ontario at the time. We always took our younger boys, Chris and Ian, to watch his games. Chris was desperate to be out on the field playing alongside his older brother. However, he was too young to sign up for the league.

From an early age, Chris had an intense passion for baseball. He would eagerly join Mark and the older kids who gathered in our court to play. His love for the sport was so deep that he would sleep with his baseball glove next to him and carry it with him everywhere. One day, during one of Mark's games, the team found themselves short a player. The coach, Warren Matheson, asked if Chris would like to step in as a substitute. Before the question was even fully asked, Chris was already grinning from ear to ear and on the field. He had an excellent game and became the go-to substitute whenever the team needed an extra player. Mark's team went on to win the championship for T-Ball that year, marking a significant achievement.

The following year, Chris was old enough to officially join the league. This was when I decided to get more involved and began coaching. Over the next 16 years, I would coach baseball at various levels. I started by coaching Chris's house league team alongside two other coaches, and we enjoyed a very successful season. After that, Chris was drafted to play on a Rep Baseball team, a touring team that competed in various cities. The Rep Team already had its coaching staff in place, so I turned my attention to coaching Mark's house league team. Under my guidance, we clinched the championship title. The following year, Mark was also drafted to the Select Team, another touring team that already had a coaching team established.

By this time, my youngest son Ian was old enough to start playing in the house league, and I took on the responsibility of coaching his team as well. Not long after, Ian was also drafted to play for Rep Baseball. At this point, I had completed my coaching courses and obtained the necessary certification to coach Rep and Select teams.

Alongside fellow coaches Monty Harkies, Chuck Lyons, and Mike McCallum, I became part of the coaching staff for Chris's Rep Team. We travelled across Ontario for various tournaments, most of which we won. By now, we had three boys playing for Rep and Select teams, all of which required extensive travel to different cities for their games. This meant a lot of coordination on our part to make sure each of them made it to their respective games. Avril and I alternated attending games, with her supporting Mark and Ian while I focused on coaching Chris's team.

For many years, our summer weekends were consumed by baseball. We spent little time at home, always on a diamond somewhere. In the process, we formed lasting friendships with other parents who were similarly devoted to the sport. To this day, we remain in touch with many of them.

The away tournaments, especially, were memorable experiences. We would book hotel rooms for the weekend, and the kids would have their own parties in one room while the parents enjoyed theirs in another. It was an exciting, bonding time for everyone involved, filled with laughter, competition, and cherished memories.

CHAPTER 31

◄─────────────•••─────────────►

From Brampton to Woodbridge: Coaching, Conflict, and Championship

    Given my deep involvement in coaching baseball, I decided to attend one of the general meetings of the Brampton Baseball Association, where various members were expressing their concerns and opinions. Feeling compelled to share my thoughts, I spoke up on one of the topics being discussed. To my surprise, Dave Dash, the president of Brampton Minor League at the time, asked if I would be interested in joining the Brampton Baseball Association Executive. I agreed and soon became part of the leadership group.

    Around the same time, a group of private investors in the neighbouring city of Mississauga built a state-of-the-art baseball dome, offering a space for players and coaches to rent to participate in a winter league. I saw an opportunity to foster collaboration and got involved with the dome's organisers. To help promote it, I invited one of their representatives to one of our executive meetings. The response was overwhelmingly positive, with several coaches expressing interest in joining the winter league. Ultimately, my team, along with others from different baseball organisations, signed up to play winter ball in the dome. The league turned out to be highly successful and provided players with an excellent opportunity to continue developing their skills during the off-season.

Within the association's executive team, various committees were formed, such as the Rep Committee, Select Committee, House League Committee, and Finance Committee. I volunteered for the Finance Committee, where I quickly noticed a troubling pattern: a family member of one of the executive board members was being paid for her involvement, even though the organisation was supposed to be entirely on a voluntary basis. I found this practice to be unethical, especially considering the community-driven nature of the organisation. This experience, along with the fact that the organisation seemed to be controlled by a single individual and a few loyal followers, left me feeling disillusioned. Many of the committee members were blue-collar workers, and for some, holding a position of power within the committee seemed to be more about gaining influence than serving the organisation's best interests.

As time went on, I wasn't the only one who became dissatisfied with how things were being run. Dr. Dale Palmer, a well-respected coach within the association, also grew frustrated with the organisation's direction. In a bold move, he, along with several other coaches, decided to leave Brampton and take an entire team with them to Woodbridge, a neighbouring city. Fortunately, or unfortunately, this included my own son, Mark.

This marked the beginning of my downfall within the association. I became the target of various accusations designed to silence me, and eventually, I was suspended from my position within the executive group. Despite this, I remained committed to the game and began attending my son's games, especially when his team competed in tournaments where Dave Dash's team was also playing. Dr. Palmer's team, which had become incredibly strong, consistently outperformed Dave's team in every tournament we participated in.

Despite the challenges I faced in Brampton Minor-Baseball, I refused to let politics ruin my passion for coaching or the bond I had built with the players, especially my sons. When Dr. Palmer stepped away from the Woodbridge team, a new chapter in my coaching journey began.

As Dr. Palmer grew busier with his professional practice, he decided to retire from coaching, and I stepped in as the new head coach for the team. I reached out to Murray Hannah, an excellent coach, and invited him to join me in coaching the team. Together, we found great success, winning most of the tournaments we entered, many of which were highly competitive events.

Our success in Woodbridge did not go unnoticed. Coaches from Brampton Minor Baseball, intrigued by our achievements, began to recruit players from Brampton to form their own teams and join us in Woodbridge. This influx of talent further elevated the level of competition and helped strengthen the baseball community in Woodbridge.

Under my leadership, our team reached the highest level of Select Baseball in Ontario, competing in the Select Ontario Baseball Association (SOBA) league. We managed to win the championship, solidifying our place as the top Select Team in the province. The other team from Brampton, which had joined us in Woodbridge, also found great success and continued to thrive.

During the winter months, many of the baseball players would often sign up for hockey, and this led to the development of some exceptional hockey players, with a few even going on to play in the NHL. However, my boys weren't particularly skilled at skating, so they weren't interested in playing hockey. Additionally, I didn't think I'd enjoy spending early mornings sitting in a cold ice rink. Instead, they chose to play indoor winter soccer, which was quite popular in the areas of Brampton and Mississauga. Both cities had excellent indoor soccer leagues that provided great opportunities for young athletes, and my boys thoroughly enjoyed their time on the field.

As I mentioned earlier, I had the privilege of coaching baseball for sixteen years, and I cherished those years immensely. It allowed me to spend a significant amount of time with my boys during their formative years. Baseball kept them focused, disciplined, and grounded, and surrounded them with friends who shared similar interests in sports. During the summer, they would often gather with their friends and head to the baseball diamond for a pickup game. Sometimes, their friends would hang out in our basement, which was equipped with a games room that had a ping pong table, air hockey, a foosball table, and a pool table.

In addition to baseball, my boys also had an interest in golf, and since we lived by a golf course, they would often head out for a round of golf. I strongly believe that kids should participate in some form of physical activity, not necessarily team sports, but anything that would help them stay focused, disciplined, and grounded.

All three of my sons eventually went to university, and looking back at the baseball teams I had coached, I'm proud to say that many of the players went on to pursue higher education, whether at a college or university. My boys had grown up now, with Mark beginning his studies at Sir Wilfrid Laurier University in Waterloo, where he was pursuing a degree in business. Chris was in his final year of high school, and Ian still had a couple more years to go before graduating from high school.

CHAPTER 32

Rising in the IT World: From My Company, AMCIAD Systems Consultant Inc. to Y2K

While I was coaching baseball, I was also working as an IT consultant. However, my contracts were through third-party headhunters, which meant a significant portion of my earnings was going to them. I quickly realised that if I operated through my own incorporated company, I could command a much higher income. This led me to take the step of incorporating my business. My kids came up with the name *AMCIAD Systems Consultant Inc.*, which represents the initials of my children: Alti, Mark, Christopher, Ian, and Avril Davis.

Once my company was officially incorporated, my first major contract was with the Provincial Ministry of Housing and Municipal Affairs. It was a highly lucrative contract as an IT consultant, where I worked on their payroll system. During my time there, I gained access to sensitive salary information and was surprised to discover that my own earnings exceeded those of some of the directors.

I ended up working with the Ministry of Housing and Municipal Affairs for nearly nine years. During this time, I built lasting friendships with colleagues, many of whom I keep in touch with today. I commuted to work via the GO Train, which was a relaxing ride, though it could be quite expensive. Nevertheless, I wasn't alone in this commute, there were hundreds of people from Brampton heading into Toronto each day, some working in my office building and others in nearby buildings downtown.

I drove a minivan at the time, and seeing an opportunity, I proposed a carpool arrangement to colleagues. I offered to drive to work, charging a fare that would help my passengers save money while also providing me with a steady extra income. My idea was met with enthusiasm, and I was able to organise a carpool for several years, making the commute more affordable for everyone while earning some extra cash.

In 1996, my dear friend Ron Austriaco, whom I had worked with for many years at the Ministry of Housing and Municipal Affairs, reached out to me with an exciting opportunity. Not only was I the godfather of his second daughter, Erica, but Ron had secured a more lucrative contract at Toronto Housing and wanted me to join him there. After careful consideration, I decided to accept his offer, which meant giving up my carpool route. Fortunately, one of my passengers, Harold Vanderhart, who also worked in the IT department at the Ministry, took over my route.

Joining Ron at Toronto Housing was a seamless transition for me. I was already highly familiar with the third-party financial software, GEAC, which we had used for years at the Ministry. At that time, GEAC was a popular financial software suite, widely used by many institutions, including banks. It covered key financial modules such as Accounts Receivable (AR), Accounts Payable (AP), and the General Ledger (GL), and I had extensive experience with it, so there was no learning curve for me at all.

My time at Toronto Housing turned out to be one of the most enjoyable and rewarding phases of my career. I made lasting friendships with many of my colleagues, including Joan Hart, with whom I remain close friends to this day. The work environment was excellent, and it was one of the most fun and exciting contracts I've had. Our office was located near the Don Valley Golf Course, which is situated near Highway 401 and Yonge Street in Toronto. Ron and I would often join fellow players such as Sal Pisani, Joe, and Mike for early morning rounds of golf. Sal, though a great coach, wasn't the best golfer, while Mike had a unique talent for hitting every tree on the course, but his scorecard somehow always showed a par or bogey. We played nine holes three mornings a week before work, and afterward, we would shower in the clubhouse and walk just two minutes down the hill to our office.

On Thursday evenings, Ron Austriaco, Joan Hart, Pat Littlejohn, and I would team up to play a full round of eighteen holes. The camaraderie among us was fantastic. Ron, Joan, and I were particularly close, often sharing lunches and dinners together. I still maintain strong friendships with Joan and her husband, Jim Hart, whom I will mention more about later in the book.

Sadly, fifteen years ago, I lost one of my best friends, Ron Austriaco. Despite the passing of my dear friend, I have stayed in touch with his wife, Anne, and their daughters, Reina and Erica, my goddaughter. Both of Ron's daughters have now completed their engineering degrees and are successfully working in their respective fields.

In Toronto, working in the IT consulting field means you're often bouncing between various companies, and as a result, your name tends to get around quite a bit.

As my company grew and my reputation in the IT sector solidified, even larger opportunities began to appear, especially with the world bracing for the Y2K scare. What came next would be one of the most memorable, lucrative, and high-pressure chapters of my career.

At the start of 1999, I received a call from a headhunter who told me that IBM was looking for someone with GEAC–GL experience to be their main point of contact at the Eaton Department Store. He asked if I was interested in the position. During that time, with the Y2K crisis looming and the turn of the century approaching, there was widespread panic. Many believed that systems would crash, elevators would freeze mid-flight, and airplanes might even fall from the sky.

I told the headhunter that I still had several months left on my current contract and wouldn't be able to take on the opportunity right away. To my surprise, he responded by asking how much I would charge to come on board. In a light-hearted manner, I jokingly told him I'd accept $80 per hour. To my astonishment, he replied, "I can guarantee you $80 an hour." That offer made me reconsider, so I went to Larry, the director of the IT department who had originally hired me, and asked if I could adjust my schedule to come in earlier and leave earlier in the evening. He agreed to the arrangement.

I called the headhunter back and confirmed I was on board. Now, I had to make it work. My days started at Toronto Housing around 7:00 AM, and I'd have lunch at my desk before heading over to the Eaton Tower on Yonge Street in Toronto, where I worked from 3:00 PM until about 10:00 PM. Given that it was the

Y2K year-end, extra hands were required, and I convinced my colleague Ron to join the team and help. IBM, which manages Eaton's IT department, had several consultants working with them. Word soon spread that Ron and I were among the highest-paid employees in the department, and with over two hundred people in the IT division, there was a fair amount of envy directed our way.

To streamline things further, Eaton also had a store at York-dale Shopping Centre, and they set up an office in the basement of that location, which made it much easier and quicker for me to travel between the two locations. Eventually, I began leaving the Eaton office earlier, as I had the flexibility to work from home. Back then, working remotely was not an issue for IT personnel. Some nights, when I had a lot of data entry to complete, I'd pay my sons $15 an hour to help out.

I'll never forget being in the office on the last day of the millennium, December 31, 1999, surrounded by coworkers, anxiously waiting to see if our systems would hold up. We kept a close eye on Australia's progress since they were twelve hours ahead of us, and when they successfully passed the Y2K test, there was a collective sigh of relief. Twelve hours later, our systems didn't experience any issues either. Looking back, as an IT professional, I do think the Y2K issue was somewhat overblown, but I certainly wasn't complaining. That year, I made over $260,000, which, adjusted for inflation, would be equivalent to approximately $496,000 today.

Eaton's Department Store, a true Canadian institution, was established in 1869 and quickly became known for its high-end offerings. However, over time, it began to lose ground to competitors such as Simpson's, Wal-Mart, and other discount stores. In addition to the increasing competition, Eaton's had also invested millions into preparing for the Y2K transition, which further strained their resources. As a result, the company found itself cutting back on its workforce, including IT consultants and even its own employees.

Around the same time, NCR, the company responsible for managing Eaton's credit card services, was looking to transition the GEAC Financial Software from Eaton's platform to its own. I was contacted by NRS, who hired me to lead the migration and installation of the software on NCR's platform. Given the short-term nature of the project, I signed a contract at an hourly rate of $120, or $1,000 per day.

CHAPTER 33

Rebuilding After Y2K: A Decade of Investing in Skills & Stocks

The Y2K crisis had prompted many businesses to spend vast amounts of money upgrading their systems, leaving little room in their budgets for system enhancements or the development of new technology. Additionally, the consulting market had become flooded with IT professionals who had left their full-time jobs to capitalise on the Y2K rush. As a result, demand for consultants had sharply decreased, and when opportunities did arise, rates had been slashed significantly.

Though I wasn't interested in taking a full-time position, as my IT career had mostly been built on contract work, I decided to wait for nine months to see if the market would recover. During this time, I took the opportunity to upgrade my skills by enrolling in ORACLE courses. I couldn't stand to stay idle, and a friend of mine asked for help with a kitchen renovation project. I took the job and made a substantial amount of money in the process. Word spread quickly about my skills in kitchen renovations, basement apartment construction, and window and door installation. Soon, I was inundated with requests for all types of renovations, from kitchens and bathrooms to basement apartments.

At the same time, I had a large house with an unfinished basement, which I decided to convert into a personal project. I built a full bar and entertainment area, along with a bedroom, kitchen, bathroom, games room, and workshop. These projects kept me extremely busy for a long time, and the work was both financially rewarding and personally fulfilling.

After months of renovations and sharpening my skills, I felt the pull back toward the corporate world. The break had been fulfilling, but I missed the structure, the energy of an office, and being part of a team. Just as I was considering re-entering the job market, an unexpected call from a headhunter led me to my next opportunity.

In October 2000, the consulting market was still struggling, and after completing the renovation of my basement, I felt it was time for a break. I had built up a network of headhunters over the years, and they frequently reached out to check on my status. One day, I received a call from a headhunter asking if I was ready to transition into a full-time position. He mentioned that TD Canada Trust was seeking a GEAC software expert, a role that caught my attention. However, I didn't respond immediately. A week later, he called again, informing me that one of the managers had reviewed my résumé and expressed a strong interest in me. He mentioned the salary offer, which was significantly lower than what I was earning as a contractor. I told him I would only consider the offer if they could increase the salary and grant me an additional week of vacation. The next day, he called back to confirm they were willing to meet my conditions. I was still uncertain, as I was hoping that the market might rebound in the new year. However,

I found myself missing the structure and routine of the corporate world, dressing up and going to the office. After some reflection, I decided to accept the offer.

On my first day, I met with my manager, who had studied at McGill University, which created an instant connection, as I had also taken a few courses there through a joint Computer Science programme with Concordia University. During our conversation, he explained that he had hired me for my technical skills, as it's easier to train a technically skilled person to handle business/accounting matters than to train someone with an accounting background to be technically proficient.

I was placed in charge of a small team of four, one of whom held a CGA designation. Together, we formed a complementary team, my technical expertise paired well with his accounting knowledge. Over time, I assumed that my manager's intention may have been to create a sort of independent IT support within the finance division. By doing this, he may have aimed to avoid being reliant on the company's main IT department, ensuring that his team could operate more efficiently and autonomously.

During my time at TD, I truly enjoyed the work environment. The people were fantastic, and I formed many lasting friendships. One of the highlights of my role was supporting the GEAC Financial software. It felt second nature to me, as I had been using it for many years. I had the opportunity to streamline several GEAC processes and improve computer procedures on a dedicated platform, enabling parallel testing of the GEAC software before production deployment. This improvement was incredibly beneficial to the department, enhancing efficiency and accuracy.

Throughout my career as a systems consultant, I worked with many companies that ran GEAC software. Nearly every one of them mentioned plans to replace it with newer technology, but interestingly, that never came to fruition. When I joined TD in 2000, they had the same intention to update their systems. Yet, even after fifteen years of working there, when I retired, GEAC was still in use, and to my knowledge, it continues to be in use today, more than a decade after my departure. No other financial system I know of could handle such a vast volume of data quite like GEAC.

Being immersed in the finance world at TD sparked a deeper interest in personal investing. Surrounded by financial experts and armed with firsthand insights into how the banking system worked, I began to manage my own investments more actively, applying what I had learned on the job.

During my time in the finance department, I gained invaluable knowledge of how banks operate and how to invest wisely. Having always managed my own investment portfolio, I took an active role in choosing stocks and mutual funds. I primarily focused on blue-chip companies and banks, as they offered stability and long-term growth potential.

One of the companies I invested in was Nortel, a massive telecommunications corporation in Canada that had been making billions of dollars in revenue. At the time, I made a significant investment in the company, believing it to be stable and well-positioned for the future. However, in 2000, the company's stock dropped by 20% after missing its revenue target for 2001. Although this was a bit of a shock, I didn't panic, assuming at the time that such a large, well-established blue-chip company would not fail and would recover. Unfortunately, the company took a turn for the worse.

In 2001, Nortel revised its sales and earnings forecast downward by half, leading to another 33% drop in its stock price. By 2002, the value of Nortel's stock had plummeted from $124.00

per share to a mere $0.47. This marked a massive loss for me, but I still maintained investments in other sectors, particularly in the banking industry.

To recover some of the losses from Nortel's collapse, I took a risk and invested in some of the rising dot-com companies. Unfortunately, this also resulted in substantial losses. However, the experience of losing significant amounts of money did not deter me from the stock market. In fact, I was doing quite well with investments in major banks such as TD Canada Trust, Scotiabank, Bank of Montreal, CIBC, and Royal Bank.

In 2008, an unusual event occurred: the Canadian Dollar (CAD) reached parity with the United States Dollar (USD). Historically, the CAD had been much weaker, sometimes 30% lower than the USD. Seeing this as an opportunity, I decided to capitalise on the foreign exchange (FX) market. I began purchasing USD when the exchange rate was favourable and waited for the CAD to decline in value. Once it did, I exchanged my USD back into CAD, successfully profiting from the fluctuations in currency values. This venture in FX trading proved to be a rewarding strategy, allowing me to recover some of my previous losses.

As I mentioned earlier in my book, I had an encounter with Mackenzie Financial, a company that Michael Lee-Chin had purchased, along with another mutual fund company, the AIC Advantage Fund, according to public knowledge, for approximately eight hundred thousand dollars ($800,000.00) in the 1980s. By the early 2000s, his investment had blossomed into something extraordinary, turning it into a multibillion-dollar enterprise. By that time, I had gained much more knowledge about investing than I had when he initially acquired Mackenzie Financial, which I had passed on investing in. I wasn't about to miss out again. This time,

I decided to invest in AIC mutual funds, and it proved to be a very lucrative decision, yielding me handsome profits.

Despite a few major setbacks in the stock market, I remained undeterred. But I also began looking at more tangible, controllable forms of investment. Real estate had always intrigued me, and with my renovation skills, I saw an opportunity to turn rundown properties into real profit.

While I was investing in the stock market with stocks and mutual funds, I also started to test my skills in the real estate market. I purchased a three-bedroom semi-detached backsplit home in Brampton, Ontario, not far from my own place. I renovated the house, transforming the basement into a self-contained two-bedroom apartment with separate entrances. This allowed me to rent it out to two families. After a while, I sold the house and made a good profit. Next, I bought a three-bedroom townhouse in Brampton that was going through foreclosure. I did a complete renovation, adding a fourth bedroom and a full bathroom. I rented it out to a lovely family who cared for the home, but after two years, they had to move because their jobs relocated them to another city.

The next tenants, however, were far less pleasant. They proved to be the "tenants from hell." Not only was it a struggle to collect rent from them, but the house quickly deteriorated under their care. Whenever I went to collect rent, they would crack the door open just a little, handing me the cheque but not allowing me to see inside. Eventually, I informed them that I would be conducting an inspection the next time I came for rent collection. On the day of the inspection, they had moved out, leaving the house in a total mess and failing to pay any rent.

When I entered the house, I was overwhelmed by the horrendous stench. The floors were covered in dog feces, and there were mice and their babies scattered across the rooms, seemingly being fed by the tenants, who had left out slices of cheese for them. Graffiti covered the glass windows, and the door casings and baseboards were chewed up by dogs. When I opened one of the cupboards, I discovered it was filled with roaches and drug paraphernalia. I didn't panic, though, because I knew that I could restore the house to its original condition. What concerned me was how Avril would react to the state of the house. I knew she would be horrified, but she insisted on seeing it despite my warnings. When she stepped inside, seeing the place in such disarray, she couldn't hold back her tears.

I hired a U-Haul truck and trailer, and enlisted the help of my two nephews, Damion and Kishawn. Together, we gutted the house, removing the windows, doors, floors, and kitchen, along with the bathrooms and some of the walls. We even installed a new furnace. After a significant amount of work, we restored the house to pristine condition, and I was able to sell it for a handsome profit. From that day forward, I made a firm resolution: I was done with the family rental business for good.

I had an investment portfolio with a close Jamaican friend who worked for Edward Jones, a prominent financial investment firm based in Canada. She had a personal connection with Michael Lee-Chin, a Jamaican billionaire a, well-known figure in both the financial and philanthropic worlds. I believe they may have even attended school together back in Jamaica. One day, she reached out to invite me to a seminar that Michael was hosting at a conference hall near Toronto Pearson International Airport. Intrigued, I decided to attend with her. The event took place in an enormous conference room that was packed with attendees. I was even surprised to spot the then-chief of the Toronto police among the crowd.

Michael Lee-Chin has made a name for himself not only for his impressive wealth but also for his generous philanthropic contributions, which are still well recognised today. Notably, he donated millions to McMaster University, where the Michael Lee-Chin & Family Institute was established, and to the Royal Ontario Museum, which boasts the iconic Michael Lee-Chin Crystal.

I vividly remember one part of his speech where he shared a piece of advice that stuck with me. He explained that true wealth isn't built by using your own money, as there's always a limit to how much you can use. Instead, he emphasised the importance of leveraging other people's money. Specifically, he encouraged the use of equity built up in your properties to fund investments.

As I listened to him, it struck me that this was exactly what I had been doing all along. Hearing this advice from a billionaire who had achieved massive success confirmed to me that I must be on the right track. The properties I had bought and sold in the past were all financed through the equity I had taken out of the house I was living in at the time.

That house was no small property, over 4,000 square feet, located by a beautiful golf course, and it had accumulated substantial equity over the years. This strategy had served me well, and hearing it endorsed by someone of Michael Lee-Chin's calibre only strengthened my belief in my approach.

As luck would have it, my real estate ventures aligned perfectly with my sons' university years. What began as a practical solution to avoid poor-quality student housing soon evolved into a highly profitable new direction for our investments.

My eldest son, Mark, enrolled at Wilfrid Laurier University in Waterloo, Ontario, which is located about an hour and a half away from Brampton. Due to the high demand for student accommodations, first-year students were allowed to live on campus for one year. After that, they were required to find their own housing. During his time on campus, Mark formed many close friendships and decided that he wanted to rent a house where he and his friends could live together.

Avril and I accompanied Mark and his friends to search for rental homes, but the properties we viewed were in poor condition. It seemed that many landlords were taking advantage of the fact that students, desperate for accommodation, were willing to accept subpar living conditions. With limited housing available, these landlords neglected the upkeep of their properties, as making repairs would incur additional costs, and many were not inclined to do the work themselves.

After viewing these rundown houses, I suggested to Avril that we consider investing in a property that Mark could live in for free, while we rented out the other rooms to his friends, generating rental income in the process. Avril was initially hesitant, worried about the debt involved in purchasing a property for this purpose. She would often remind me that her father had always avoided debt, preferring to pay for everything in cash.

In contrast, my upbringing was quite different. Growing up, my family didn't always have the money to pay for everything in cash. As a result, my parents would arrange with shop owners to keep a running tab for purchases and would settle the balance at a later date when they had the money. In Jamaica, this system was referred to as "Trust." I recall running errands for my mother, walking into the local shop, and calling out to the shopkeeper, "Miss Jill, please trust me, 1 pound of flour, 2 pounds of sugar, and half a pound of salt fish." She would add it to my mother's tab, knowing her well.

After much persuasion, I was able to convince Avril that this was an excellent and lucrative opportunity. With the substantial equity we had built up in our home, coming up with the required down payment wasn't a challenge. The bank only required a 25% down payment for investment properties, which was easily within reach.

Once everything was in motion, we decided to act. I created a flyer announcing that I was looking to purchase a property in the area, and we distributed them throughout the neighbourhood near the university. Our efforts paid off when we received a response from a potential seller. By this time, Avril had obtained her real estate licence, which meant we could save on commission fees when purchasing the property.

The house we found was perfect. It featured three self-contained apartments, each with its own separate entrance. The basement contained a three-bedroom apartment, the main floor had another three-bedroom unit, and the third floor housed a two-bedroom apartment. Each apartment had its own kitchen and common area, making it an ideal property for rental income. I took on the task of fully renovating the entire house, and once completed, Mark and his friends moved in.

The following year, my second son, Chris, enrolled at Brock University in St. Catharine's, Ontario. Seeing an opportunity, I purchased a five-bedroom duplex in the area. Although Chris didn't live there, I rented out the units to five students, ensuring the property generated some income.

The year after that, my youngest son, Ian, began his studies at McMaster University in Hamilton, Ontario. By this point, I had three sons in university, which meant there was a significant amount of tuition and expenses to cover. To help ease the financial burden, we followed the same approach we had taken for

Mark. We took Ian and five of his friends, three girls and two boys, on a house-hunting trip. Eventually, we found a charming one-and-a-half-storey house with an unfinished basement. I purchased the property and immediately began construction to add three bedrooms and a second bathroom in the basement. Ian and his friends moved in as soon as the renovations were completed.

The following year, I noticed that McMaster University was experiencing rapid growth in its student population, and I recognised an opportunity in purchasing more properties near the university, which had become highly lucrative. I still had a significant amount of equity from the home I was living in, and the 11-bedroom house I had bought in Waterloo for my son, Mark, had also appreciated considerably.

By this time, Avril had become more comfortable with the idea of investing in real estate, so we decided to explore more opportunities in the area. We began looking for houses not too far from the McMaster campus. Ian, who had always been interested in real estate, was eager to join us on our house-hunting journey.

We viewed several properties, but Avril, who had recently become a licensed real estate agent, tended to focus on the disarray and poor condition of many houses. On the other hand, Ian and I were able to look past the mess and potential issues. We were primarily concerned with the structural integrity of the homes, and as long as the foundation and framework were sound, we were confident in moving forward with the purchase.

Eventually, we bought a spacious six-bedroom, two-storey house that was just a few minutes' walk from the McMaster campus. It had two bathrooms, a kitchen, and a living room, which made it ideal for student rentals. True to form, I set about renovating the house, as I had with all the properties I had previously acquired.

While we were working on our newly acquired property, we noticed that the owner of a similar house next door was also undertaking a renovation project. He was aware that we had purchased the house with plans to rent it to students, and one day, as we were working on our own property, he approached us to see if we might be interested in buying his house as well. Without hesitation, we agreed to consider his offer if the price was right. It turned out that the price was indeed favourable for us, so Avril quickly drafted the offer, and we purchased the property privately, bypassing real estate agent commission fees.

These types of houses were in high demand for student rentals due to their proximity to McMaster University, making them excellent investments in the growing rental market.

In 2006, after seeing the impressive income from our student rental properties, we decided to expand our portfolio and look for another student property. We found a duplex located a bit farther from the university, but it was very popular with graduate students, so we decided to purchase it. The duplex had two separate living units, each with two large bedrooms. Wanting to maximise the property's potential, I converted both units by adding a third bedroom in each, making them three-bedroom apartments.

While I was eager to buy even more properties, Avril had to step in and hold me back. It became clear that student rentals were far more profitable and less stressful than managing family rental properties. I no longer had to worry about chasing rent payments since the students' parents were covering them. And while the tenants were rarely a cause for concern in terms of damaging the property, they weren't exactly the cleanest. Male students seemed content living in a mess, which didn't bother me too much. When they moved out, I would simply give the house a good cleaning before the next group of tenants arrived.

The most frequent calls I received were from houses with all-female tenants. In these situations, I often found myself acting as a "parent away from home," helping resolve conflicts between the girls. There were a few instances where the students called with what seemed like major issues. For example, I received one call about a light not working. When I enquired if they had tried changing the light bulb, the response was, "Ah, that's why." I reminded myself that these were eighteen- and nineteen-year-old girls who had just left home and were still adjusting to handling simple household tasks without their parents' assistance.

In contrast, houses with all-male tenants typically generated fewer calls, as the guys would wait until the very last light bulb blew out before reaching out to me. However, the male students were, by far, the least tidy group.

The ideal setup, in my experience, was a mixed-gender group of tenants. The girls would generally keep the house cleaner and were often the ones to ask the boys for help when repairs were needed, striking a balance that worked well for everyone involved.

CHAPTER 34

Building a Legacy: From Renovations to Real Estate Empire

While I was simultaneously managing the purchase and renovation of several properties, I still held down a full-time, nine-to-five job at the bank. The workload was often overwhelming, and there were times when I worked well past midnight, only to drive back home to Brampton afterward. The fatigue was draining, so when I had large-scale renovations underway, I would stay at the various properties to make commuting more manageable. I'd travel directly from there to work each day. On weekends, Avril and I would pack an air mattress and spend the entire weekend at whichever house we were focusing on.

Avril was truly the ultimate renovation partner, unfailingly reliable and hardworking. She never once complained; she simply dove into whatever task needed attention. She had honed her painting skills during our time in Montreal when I was attending university. Back then, she would often join me on painting projects at the various properties I was working on. By this point, she had become a seasoned expert in painting, and while I tackled the more intense aspects of the renovations, she took charge of all the painting work.

Owning multiple properties, renovating them, and balancing the demands of a full-time job were undeniably exhausting. There were days when, during lunch breaks at the bank, I would walk over to the nearby Sheraton Hotel, find a quiet spot in the lobby, and sit down to eat. Afterward, I'd set my phone alarm for a quick half-hour nap. Those moments of rest were a much-needed recharge that kept me going.

When I was heavily investing in properties, I encouraged several of my friends to get involved as well. However, most of them were hesitant, and one friend even told me that it would be wiser for him to focus on paying off the mortgage on his house instead. As far as I know, his mortgage is now paid off, but he continues to live in the same house. It seems that investment opportunities aren't suited for everyone.

As Avril and I powered through renovations and late nights, balancing work and property projects, life at home was changing too. Our sons were growing up fast, finding their own paths in the world. Watching them leave for university, chart their futures, and even invest in real estate themselves brought a new layer of purpose to everything we'd been building.

My three sons completed their studies at university. My eldest son, Mark, pursued a business degree at Sir Wilfrid Laurier University.

After university, he decided to embark on a journey of exploration, and with his friend Andrew Davis (no relation), he travelled to London, England. There, they worked while using the city as a base for some travels throughout Europe. After a year,

Andrew returned to Canada to pursue a career in medicine and became a medical doctor. Mark, however, decided to stay in London. He worked for several companies before being hired by Network Rail as a trainee manager for the role of Quantitative Surveyor. Network Rail is responsible for owning, operating, maintaining, and developing Britain's railways. The company supported Mark in furthering his education by funding his master's degree, prompting him to remain with them for some time while continuing to explore Europe. He has since moved on to become a director at a consulting company that Network Rail hires.

My youngest son, Ian, also pursued a business degree, this time at McMaster University. He, along with his girlfriend Alanna Boyle, now his wife, followed in Mark's footsteps and decided to travel to London, England. Ian worked his way into a role in production at the BBC before moving on to a year-long position with FOX Television in Sydney, Australia. Over the years, he's had the opportunity to travel to over 60 countries. Today, Ian is a senior manager at TSN Sports Television in Canada, where his career continues to thrive.

As for my middle son, Chris, he chose a different path and earned an accounting degree at Brock University in St. Catharine's, Ontario. Following in my footsteps, he decided to invest in real estate, purchasing a couple of student properties near Brock University. After beginning his career, Chris currently works as a Forensic Accountant with an insurance company, specialising in business interruption cases. It's fulfilling to see all my sons chart their own unique paths, and I couldn't be prouder of the journeys they've taken.

When I first pitched the idea of investing in real estate to my friends, only a few showed interest. One of the people who did, however, was my coworker, Anh Phan, whom I'll now refer to as my first financial student. Anh, who had once been one of my staff members, was eager to learn. I sat down with her and shared my approach to using the equity in her home to her advantage, explaining how she could tap into the value of her property and make it work for her. Anh and I shared something in common beyond just a professional connection. We are both immigrants. Anh was one of the Vietnamese Boat People who came to Canada seeking a better life. Inspired by my approach to real estate investment, Anh followed a similar path and, like me, went on to build substantial wealth. Today, she is a multi-millionaire.

With our sons thriving and even some of my coworkers following in our footsteps to build wealth through property, I felt confident in the direction our lives were heading. But I wasn't done yet. A new opportunity was brewing, this time far from Canada, in the sun-soaked neighbourhoods of Florida, where a market crash had created a once-in-a-lifetime chance to expand our vision beyond borders.

In 2008, when the U.S. housing market collapsed due to the housing bubble bursting, it devastated many people, including my brother Valin. He owned multiple properties in Florida and Georgia, and the crash significantly affected his investments. I began closely monitoring the U.S. housing market, and by 2010, when property prices hit rock bottom, I saw an opportunity and jumped on it without hesitation, like a lion pouncing on its prey.

I reached out to several real estate agents in Florida, inquiring about the deeply discounted properties available. However, most of them never responded to my queries. They were still clinging to the hope that the market was just experiencing a temporary setback and that prices would rise again, along with their commissions. Chester Freels, one of the few agents who replied, was quick to send me a list of available properties.

Excited by the possibilities, Avril and I reviewed the listings and decided to meet Chester. We flew down to Florida, staying at my brother Valin's home in Miramar, and connected with Chester. He took us to various cities in Broward County to tour properties. The experience was exhilarating, almost like a child in a candy store, excitedly picking out what they wanted. Avril had to keep me grounded as I eagerly pointed out which properties I wanted to invest in.

We were prepared to make all our purchases in cash, having built up significant equity in our Canadian properties over the years. Once the deals were finalised, we returned to Canada, thrilled by the investment opportunities we had secured.

Naturally, I couldn't wait to share my success with others. I was passionately telling anyone who would listen about the benefits of buying properties in Florida, just as I had done when investing in student houses. My son, Chris, was especially excited. The very next month, he and I flew back to Florida. We met up with Chester again, and Chris bought a couple of properties while I acquired a few more. Afterward, we returned to Canada, still excited and sharing the word about our Florida real estate investments.

One of my colleagues kept telling me he was going to make the investment too, but he never followed through. As I've said before, property investment is not for everyone. However, another coworker, Geeta Galani, was intrigued. Like I had done with Anh, I took the time to explain the process to Geeta in detail. She contacted Chester, flew down to Florida, and purchased a couple of properties. Eventually, Geeta owned five properties in Florida.

By now, we had built up quite a portfolio of properties in Florida, but both Chris and I were still eager for more. At this point, we had developed a strong relationship with our realtor,

Chester, and we trusted him to handle the purchases even when we weren't physically present. Whenever we found a property we liked, we simply called him to get his honest opinion, and if it seemed like a good fit, he would handle the purchase on our behalf. This approach saved us from having to fly back and forth to Florida every time we wanted to purchase a property. Both Chris and I continued to acquire several properties this way, further expanding our portfolios without ever having to leave home.

Some of these properties needed some work done to them, so Avril and I would fly down to Florida and hire my brother Valin on occasion to help whenever he was available.

The employment market was bad around that time in the United States as well, so whenever you drove by any Home Depot store, there were always a huge number of people, mostly men, looking for work.

It was quite easy to get local tenants, as there was a demand for rental properties since people had lost their homes to foreclosures and had nowhere to live.

While we were down there doing the renovations, Chester, our real estate agent and now a friend, came and told us that he had found a property and that we should have a look at it.

The moment we walked through the front door, we said yes. This condo overlooked a beautifully kept golf course with a lake, and it was on the ninth floor. You could see the beautiful Palm Aire Complex, and not far away was the very popular Isles Casino and harness racetrack.

Avril read through the condo rules, and it stated that the condo was not allowed to be rented for the first two years of owning it.

Avril pointed this out to Chester. He looked at us and said he thought that after we had bought all these properties, we should have one for ourselves. At the time, it had never occurred to us to get a place for ourselves, as we still had full-time jobs and were not ready for retirement.

The previous owner had bought it for two hundred and seventy-five thousand dollars ($275,000.00) and had to foreclose for sixty-eight thousand dollars ($68,000.00).

To us, it was the bargain of the century, so we purchased it.

Avril and I took a week off from work, flew down to Florida, and started a full renovation of the condo. It was somewhat dated, with some old tiles on the balcony, and the entire apartment floor was carpeted, as it was the norm in Florida to carpet or put down ceramic flooring.

We decided to rip it all out and replace it with laminate flooring, and while I was replacing the flooring, Avril was on the balcony with her hammer and chisel, removing the old ceramic tiles. We also changed all the doors and light fixtures, and then completely repainted it.

After the renovations were completed, Avril was very happy and eager to furnish the apartment. I was dragged around several furniture stores looking for furniture, and at the completion of the furniture-buying spree, the condo was beautifully furnished.

We still had our full-time jobs and were not ready for retirement, so we were not able to spend a lot of time there.

During that time, Spirit Airlines was doing daily flights out of Niagara Falls, USA, to Fort Lauderdale, Florida. This was a budget airline, leaving Niagara Falls at midnight for a three-hour flight to Fort Lauderdale. The airfares were unbelievably cheap. We could buy a return ticket to Fort Lauderdale for as little as sixty US dollars ($60.00 USD), and this airline was very popular with Ontarians, who would flock over the border to capitalise on these cheap airfares. With these cheap airline fares, we flew down regularly for extended weekends. Our sons and their partners, as well as some friends, enjoyed the use of the condo as well.

At this point, a couple of friends, Jim Hart and Don Clark, whom I had previously talked to about my recent property purchases in Florida, reached out to me to get a better understanding of buying real estate in Florida. Jim and I had been friends for many years, largely due to my work with his wife, Joan Hart, whom I met on one of my IT contracts with Metro/Toronto Housing. Jim Hart had a distinguished career with the City of Toronto, where he held several prominent positions, including Executive Director of Municipal Licensing and Standards, General Manager of Parks, Forestry and Recreation, Toronto City Councillor, and Chair of the Toronto Police Services Board.

I was also good friends with Don and Nela Clark, and I had the honour of attending their wedding. Avril, my wife, met Nela while they were both training to become real estate agents, and Don and I bonded over our shared appreciation of handyman work. As a result of our friendship, I introduced both Jim and Don to Chester, our trusted real estate agent in Florida. They travelled down to Florida separately, not knowing each other at the time, but later connected through me. Jim purchased two condos, while Don acquired several.

I was managing a total of fifteen properties while still working a demanding nine-to-five job. Around this time, one of my staff members, Lesley Stelling, who had worked for TD Bank for over 40 years, was thinking of retiring. With her retirement, all her responsibilities would be handed over to me, which made me start seriously thinking about my own early retirement. Although retiring meant giving up a significant salary, I realised I could afford to take that step. More importantly, it would grant me the freedom to do whatever I wanted, without being constrained by the demands of work. One of my lifelong dreams was to travel, and early retirement would give me the opportunity to finally pursue that passion.

CHAPTER 35

We flew to Fiji and Sydney, Australia, to visit our son Ian and his girlfriend, Alanna.

My son Ian and his girlfriend Alanna, who had been living in London, England, for over seven years, made the decision to return to Canada. However, before coming back home, they told us that they wanted to spend a year in Australia. Avril and I were absolutely thrilled by this news, as both of us had always dreamed of travelling to Australia to experience the unique culture of the people "down under." Seizing the opportunity, we decided to visit them during their time there.

As we planned our trip, we thought it would be a fantastic idea to make a stopover in Fiji. Not only would it give us a chance to explore the beautiful islands, but it would also break up the lengthy 20-hour flight to Sydney, where Ian and Alanna were living. When we mentioned our plan to stop in Fiji, Ian and Alanna decided to meet us there, which made the trip even more exciting.

In November 2014, Avril and I flew from Toronto Pearson International Airport to Los Angeles International Airport, where we had an eight-hour layover before our flight to Fiji. We made the most of this by exploring a few notable places in Los Angeles. One of our stops was Venice Beach, where we were completely taken aback by the living conditions of the homeless people there. The scene we encountered was unlike anything I had ever seen before, even in Jamaica, where I was born, a country often labelled as a Third World nation.

The entire boardwalk was lined with people living in makeshift homes, using old, dilapidated indoor furniture and covered with tattered tarps that were blowing in the wind. It was a stark and eye-opening contrast, and the experience left a lasting impression on both of us.

We took a long flight from LAX to Fiji, which lasted about twelve hours, finally arriving at our hotel, where Ian and Alanna had already arrived the day before. Little did we know they had a big surprise waiting for us: Alanna was wearing her engagement ring. The thought that they might be engaged never crossed my mind, even though they had been in a relationship for about eight to nine years. When we met them at the hotel, I noticed that Alanna kept gesturing with her hand as she spoke to us. I, being completely oblivious to such things, didn't realise why she was doing this until Avril suddenly screamed, "Congratulations!" That's when I finally understood that Ian and Alanna had just gotten engaged.

Fiji is made up of over three hundred islands, and during our trip, we took a cruise from the main island, visiting several smaller islands along the way. While cruising on the catamaran, which had about twenty-five passengers aboard, we often saw smaller boats pulling up beside us to transfer goods to the islands.

One of the highlights of the trip was visiting a local school. Avril and I, having been teachers in Jamaica, were particularly excited to experience this, and the children were equally enthusiastic. We took plenty of pictures with them, capturing the special moment.

Being in Fiji felt like being home in Jamaica, especially because the islands had many of the same fruits I grew up eating: mangoes, coconuts, breadfruits, and bananas. The people of Fiji left a lasting impression on me; they are incredibly friendly and welcoming. During my stay at the hotel, I often looked out for the local staff during their breaks to chat. Some nights, I even joined the men on the beach as they gathered around in a circle to drink Kava, a traditional Fijian drink made from local roots. The men wore traditional attire, which included a skirt-like dress. When we visited the school, some of the male teachers were dressed in these dresses, paired with a tie, and they looked fantastic.

One day, as Avril, Ian, Alanna, and I were walking along the beach, we saw a young man riding a horse. In a spontaneous moment of fun, I challenged him and his horse to a race. The race along the beach turned into a thrilling spectacle, and I think I created an exciting moment for everyone who was watching as the horse and I raced at full speed across the sand.

We also had the opportunity to visit a village hall, where we sat in a circle with the chief. Our feet were crossed in front of us as we drank Kava, which is said to have intoxicating effects if consumed in excess. It was a unique and memorable cultural experience that gave us a deeper appreciation of Fijian traditions.

All in all, our time in Fiji was unforgettable. We spent a week enjoying the islands before flying off to Sydney for the next part of our adventure.

Ian and Alanna's apartment was just a short three-minute walk from Bondi Beach. While they were at work, Avril and I would often stroll down to the beach to unwind, enjoy a few drinks at the local bar, and watch the surfers do their thing in the waves.

During their time in England, Ian and Alanna had become close friends with several Australians and New Zealanders. It's quite common for people from these countries to spend a couple of years in the UK before returning home. Although these friends had since moved back to Australia and New Zealand, they had settled in different cities across both countries.

Before Avril and I flew to Australia, Alanna had been secretly planning a surprise birthday celebration for Ian. The logistics of coordinating such an event proved challenging, as many of their friends were spread out across various countries and cities. But Alanna pulled it off brilliantly. She managed to contact all their friends, both in Australia and New Zealand, and had them mark the date on their calendars. Ian's friends from Melbourne, Cairns, and New Zealand flew in the night before the party.

The plan was for Avril, Alanna, and I to take Ian to one of the restaurants and bars along Bondi Beach to celebrate his birthday. Bondi Beach is lined with several excellent dining and drinking spots, so we chose one of the nicer ones. After ordering our drinks, we relaxed and chatted. Completely unknown to Ian, his friends were already on their way.

Without Ian suspecting a thing, his friends suddenly burst into the restaurant shouting, "SURPRISE!" Ian was completely stunned, his face filled with disbelief as he had no idea this was coming. Alanna had done an incredible job pulling off the surprise, keeping everything under wraps until that very moment.

189

We spent the evening enjoying the company of his friends, many of whom we had met during our visits to England and during their trips to our home in Canada. Afterward, we returned to Ian and Alanna's apartment for more drinks and continued the celebration late into the night.

Avril and I had always wanted to explore more of Australia, and we had heard wonderful things about the Gold Coast, renowned for its natural beauty. While staying at Ian and Alanna's apartment, his Australian friends put together a travel itinerary for us, suggesting some must-see destinations. We flew into Brisbane, where we rented a car and spent some time touring the city before driving to Noosa, a stunning spot located on Queensland's Sunshine Coast. Noosa is celebrated for its beautiful, sunny weather and pristine beaches, which make it the perfect destination. We checked into a hotel there, which would serve as our base for further adventures.

One of the highlights was booking a safari-like tour that picked us up from the hotel and took us to the rainforest on Fraser Island. Known as the largest sand island in the world, Fraser Island is home to towering, majestic trees growing right in the sand. Inland, we explored freshwater dune lakes, and we were lucky enough to spot some dingoes walking along the beach, a rare and exciting sight.

The drive to Fraser Island took a couple of hours, and though I was eager to witness kangaroos hopping around in the fields, perhaps even boxing and kicking as they sometimes do in the wild, our hopes were dashed. We only encountered about four young kangaroos grazing peacefully in the fields, and that was the extent of our kangaroo sightings during our entire three-week trip across Australia.

We arrived at Fraser Island around midday and wasted no time diving into a crystal-clear, freshwater lake. Honestly, it was the clearest lake I had ever seen. After a refreshing swim, we gathered with other tour groups at a designated area where a barbecue lunch was served. I opted for a steak, which seemed to be a popular choice among fellow travellers. However, as we ate, the tour operators had to constantly shoo away the Laughing Kookaburras, who were intent on snatching food from the tables. Unfortunately, I was one of the unlucky ones. Out of nowhere, a Kookaburra swooped down and stole my steak! Thankfully, the camaraderie among tour operators meant that another one quickly replaced my meal with another steak.

On our journey to Fraser Island, it took us a couple of hours to get there. However, on the way back to Noosa, the journey took on a unique twist. As the tide receded, the beach became a makeshift highway, stretching for seventy miles. It was fascinating to witness cars driving along the beach, with beachgoers casually strolling or swimming near the shore while vehicles zipped just a few feet away. It took half the time to get back to Noosa.

Upon our return to Noosa, we came across flyers promoting a concert by a well-known reggae band from New Zealand, performing in a small town called Kin Kin. The town, nestled in the rolling hills, also had an old country pub called Pomona. We decided to make the drive to the concert, which was packed with an energetic crowd. I was the only Black person in the venue, aside from one of the band members, and I had never seen so many white Rastafarians with dreadlocks in one place. During an intermission, one of the band members approached me; perhaps he thought we might share something in common, aside from the fact that I was the only Black person in the audience. When I mentioned I was Jamaican, he was thrilled and told me that the band's bass player and music arranger was also from Kingston, Jamaica. He took me backstage to meet him, and we instantly connected, speaking in our Jamaican patois. The other members of the band couldn't quite follow our conversation, but we enjoyed reminiscing about home. The bassist was only with the band for tours, handling the bass and music arrangements, so it was a unique chance to meet him.

Our time in Noosa was unforgettable, and after some great days exploring, we drove back to Brisbane, returned our rental car, and flew back to Sydney. In Sydney, we continued our adventures with Ian and Alanna. We visited the iconic Sydney Opera House, took a ferry to Manly Beach, and enjoyed drinks and dinner with some of Ian's friends.

Ian had purchased a car while living in Australia, planning to use it for travelling before he left. However, the car's brakes needed changing, so we drove to the auto shop to buy the necessary parts. I showed Ian how to replace the brakes himself, and by the end of it, he was equipped with the skills to take care of his car maintenance on his own. It was a fitting end to our Australian adventure, and I was glad to have been able to help him out.

We had an unforgettable time in Australia with Ian and Alanna, experiencing everything we had hoped for. However, as much as we enjoyed our time there, the moment had come for us to head back home. During our stay, Ian and Alanna had started selling off furniture and other items they had accumulated over the year they spent living in Australia. As they were preparing for their upcoming travels through South Korea, China, Vietnam, Cambodia, and other destinations on their way home, we helped them by taking back several souvenirs for them.

Ian kindly drove us to the airport, where we bid each other farewell. We then flew to Fiji, where we transferred to an Air Fiji flight that took us to Los Angeles (LAX), and from there, we finally made our way back to Toronto. Though Avril and I were eager to explore more of the world, I had a full-time job, and that was when I began considering the idea of early retirement. I longed to spend more time travelling while also focusing on the upkeep and management of my properties.

CHAPTER 36

I made up my mind to take early retirement.

By the time our trip to Australia ended, I had made up my mind: early retirement was the path I would take. Throughout my career, I have been consulting in IT for numerous companies, including IBM, McKenzie Financial, McDonnell Douglas, Trans Canada Credit, Provincial Housing, Toronto Housing, and EATON stores. Over the years, I earned a significant income and made savvy investments in the stock market.

When I took a position at TD Canada Trust in the year 2000, I initially hoped it would be a temporary stint, as I was anticipating a rebound in the consulting market. While it did recover to some extent, it never quite reached the billing rates I had previously commanded. During my time at TD, I formed lasting friendships, and my immediate boss, Kim Brown was exceptional, which made me rethink my decision to leave.

I found myself enjoying my work, particularly because I was well-versed in GEAC financial systems, having worked with the same system across various companies over the years. My office was located on the 30th floor, offering an incredible view of Centre Island, the Sky Dome, CN Tower, and Lake Ontario; it was truly the best view imaginable. During lunch breaks, I often took strolls to the waterfront, where I'd sit on a bench, watching tourists leisurely wander by. On occasion, I would walk along the boardwalk and be asked by tourists to use their cameras or phones to take pictures of them, adding a small but pleasant touch to my day.

TD made it an enjoyable experience for employees by organising various events such as boat cruises on Lake Ontario, picnics on Centre Island, baseball games, a day at Ontario Place, regular lunch gatherings, and unforgettable Christmas parties. These activities created a fun, engaging atmosphere at work.

As I mentioned previously, I had been contemplating early retirement, but there was no immediate pressure to act on it. That changed when Lesley Stelling, one of the team members I managed, who had been with TD for 40 years, finally submitted her retirement letter. I knew that with a company-wide budget freeze in place, they wouldn't be hiring a replacement for her, and all her responsibilities would be shifted to me. After discussing the situation with Avril, we both agreed that the time had come for me to retire.

Although I was about to forgo a six-figure income, the financial impact wasn't as severe as one might think. I had been reporting a substantial amount of revenue to the Canada Revenue Agency (CRA) due to my rental properties. Without the high salary, my taxable income would decrease, which would ultimately lower my tax bracket, easing the financial transition.

In 2015, after 15 years of service at TD Canada Trust, I submitted my retirement letter to my Vice President. Saying goodbye to my colleagues was difficult, as I had grown close to many of them during my time at the bank. To mark the occasion, my department threw a farewell party, which Avril attended to show her support.

Retirement granted me the freedom to travel as much as I wished, and we now have the luxury of spending our winter months at our condo in Florida. Since retiring, I've maintained close relationships with former colleagues; some are also retired, while others continue to work. We regularly meet for lunch and drinks twice a year, keeping our bond alive.

Looking back, retirement has been one of the best decisions I've ever made. There's no pressure to rush to get tasks done, and I now have the time to focus on things that matter to me. Managing and working on my properties has become a true passion, and having the time to do so has been incredibly rewarding.

Early retirement brought the freedom I had always longed for, but it also forced Avril and I to take a hard look at how we were living. With our sons grown and gone, and our days no longer dictated by work, we began to consider whether it was time to make another major life change, one that would challenge our attachment to the home we had built our lives around.

Now my three sons had already graduated from university and had moved out of our spacious 4,000 square-foot home, which had once been filled with energy, but now it was just Avril, our two cats, and I living in it. After the boys left, Avril had been urging me for months to consider downsizing to a smaller home.

I had a deep attachment to this house. Not only was it large and beautifully situated in a prime location, but it also represented years of hard work and personal investment. I had built an entertainment centre and a wet bar in the basement, making it the perfect space for gatherings. This was the cherished family home where my mother, siblings, extended relatives, and close friends came together year after year to celebrate Christmas, Easter, and Thanksgiving. It was more than just a house; it was the heart of our family traditions. During these special gatherings, the rooms would come alive with laughter, storytelling, and the warm comfort of shared memories. We would reminisce about the past while sipping glasses of wine and enjoying generous plates of delicious food, lovingly prepared and served. Dishes like curried goat, roast turkey, and tender oxtail were staples on our holiday table, bringing both nourishment and a deep sense of connection to our heritage. These moments, rich with love and togetherness, are etched in my heart as some of the most meaningful of my life. The house was located on Westchester Estate, by the Peel Village golf course in Brampton, Ontario. I often spent my leisure time playing golf there, which added to my fondness for the house.

Growing up in Jamaica, it was always my dream to be successful and own a large house. In the affluent part of Upton, Ocho Rios, near the golf course, there were grand houses owned by wealthy white Europeans and Americans, complete with swimming pools. I lived on the poor side of town, in a humble area, and often dreamed of one day owning such a large home. So, for me, selling this house and moving to a much smaller one was a difficult decision. Avril, on the other hand, found the idea much easier to accept. Coming from York, England, where larger homes were not the norm, she had a different perspective on the significance of living in a big house.

We also owned several student rental properties in Hamilton, Ontario, including one in a lovely residential area called Princes Point in Westdale Village, just a short five-minute walk to Lake Ontario. However, during the winter months, it became more challenging to rent out the house to students, as it was not a short walk to McMaster University.

Ultimately, Avril managed to convince me to sell our large house in Brampton and move to the more compact home in Hamilton. Despite the appeal of the new location, I had many concerns about downsizing. My garage was filled with valuable items, including the kit car I built in 1983, along with numerous car parts for Mercedes-Benz, Jaguar, and VW Beetles. Additionally, my basement workshop housed a large table saw, an air compressor, and various tools that I often relied on for projects.

There was storage space at our other properties in Hamilton. One property had a shed where the car could be stored, and another had an unfinished basement for car parts. The real issue for me was the loss of space for my larger projects. I couldn't imagine doing work on such a scale in a smaller space.

To resolve the situation, I proposed a compromise: If the city of Hamilton allowed me to build a garage, I would consider making the move. I visited the city planning office and was pleased to learn that they would approve the construction, as they were encouraging residents to take cars off the streets. This gave me the reassurance I needed to proceed with the downsizing.

We made the decision to sell our primary home, but we knew that there was a significant amount of work required before we could settle into our once-student house in Hamilton. The house, built in 1943, needed a complete overhaul. Our vision for the house was to renovate it entirely, modernising it to reflect our style while maintaining its charm. We also saw an opportunity to increase the value of our current home by making a few key modifications. One of the most impactful changes I planned was to install a second kitchen in the basement and add a separate side entrance to the basement, which we knew would be an attractive selling point.

A few years earlier, I had already replaced the roof on our current home, so it was in excellent condition. However, my immediate focus shifted to the Hamilton house, as it was completely empty after the students had moved out, and I hadn't re-rented it. The first step was to completely gut the house, removing the kitchen, bathrooms, all the flooring, windows & doors, and stripping the drywall down to the studs. Once the house was stripped down, I began replacing all the windows with modern double-glazed ones to improve insulation and energy efficiency. Since the house was built without any insulation in the walls, I added new insulation and replaced the old drywall.

In the kitchen and bathrooms, I installed ceramic tiles, while the rest of the house got beautiful hardwood flooring. The final step was to repaint the entire house, giving it a fresh, modern look. Avril took on the task of painting, and her work truly made the house look brand new. The entire renovation took about two months to complete, and though it was mostly a solo effort, Avril was a huge help, especially with the painting. The only part I didn't handle was the kitchen cabinets, which my good friend Don Clark, Nela's husband, installed for me as he worked for a kitchen company and got me a good discount.

Once the Hamilton house was fully renovated, it was time to tackle the next big project: renovating our current home. This was another massive undertaking, but installing a second kitchen in the basement seemed straightforward to me since I had experience constructing kitchens and installing cabinets. The roofing, however, was a much bigger challenge. A few years earlier, when we had decided to replace the roof, Avril had convinced me to hire professional roofers, who would have completed the job in a day with ten workers. However, the cost would have been $15,000, which I felt was excessive.

As luck would have it, the roofers didn't show up on the scheduled day, either because it was a busy season for roofers, or perhaps I made an error with the scheduling (wink, wink). Instead of waiting, I decided to take on the task myself. The roof had three dormers, and the house itself was large, spanning 4,000 square feet. I measured the roof, took the measurements to the shingle company, and arranged for them to deliver the shingles using a crane to place them on various sections of the roof.

Equipped with safety harnesses and ropes, I climbed to the top and began stripping the old shingles, replacing them one section at a time. It was a monumental job, and every day, neighbours and golfers passing by would stop and watch. One onlooker even remarked, "You're either brave or stupid to take on a task like this." It took me an entire week to complete the roof. The materials cost around $5,000. The $10,000 I saved by doing the work myself went toward an all-inclusive trip to Jamaica for me, Avril, and our three sons, along with their girlfriends, a much-needed family getaway.

By taking on these massive renovation projects ourselves, we not only transformed two homes but also saved a substantial amount of money that we could invest elsewhere.

The most significant challenge of the project was yet to come: constructing a side entrance to the basement. To achieve this, I needed to dig eight feet down to the house foundation, creating an opening that would measure twelve feet in length and eight feet in width. This would require removing all the soil by hand, using only a pickaxe and shovel. After carefully planning, I submitted a request to the utility companies to have the gas, electricity, and water lines located, ensuring I wouldn't accidentally disrupt them during the excavation process.

Although hiring an excavation company would have expedited the task, the quotes I received were prohibitively expensive. I've never been one to shy away from hard work, and I was determined to handle the job myself. Throughout all my home renovation projects, I've always taken a hands-on approach, sometimes with the help of my assistant, Avril.

I'm quite skilled in a variety of trades, having personally handled all of the electrical, plumbing, appliance repair, flooring, carpentry, window installation, and even roofing work for my home renovations.

The excavation itself took me about four days. Each day, I manually loaded the soil into my truck and made several trips at night to a construction site where I could dump it. Afterward, I rented a concrete saw to cut through the twelve-inch concrete wall that would form the door opening to the basement. This task took me a couple of days to complete. Once the opening was prepared, my next step was to build the retaining wall and stairs that would lead down to the basement door. This took about a week of work. In total, the entire project took me over a month to complete.

As the saying goes, hindsight is 20/20. If we had sold the house just one year later, we would have likely doubled the selling price, as the real estate market saw an extraordinary surge in property values. We had lived in that house for many years, and over time, we accumulated a great deal of belongings. Among them were several car engines and parts that I had brought with me from Montreal nearly three decades ago. At the time, I had planned to rebuild those engines as a hobby, but life got in the way, and I never got around to working on them.

We were moving from a large 4,000-square-foot home to a much smaller 1,400-square-foot house. Naturally, much of our old furniture wouldn't fit into the new space. Avril made the decision that we wouldn't bring any of the furniture with us. Instead, we would furnish the new house entirely with new pieces.

To make the transition easier, I invited family members to stop by and take whatever furniture they wanted. Whatever was left, I donated to Goodwill, and some pieces were put out on the curb, where they were quickly claimed by neighbours. The remaining items to be moved included my office desk, cabinets, clothes, and a mountain of tools and parts from my workshop and garage.

On the day of the move, our friend Nela Clark came to help us pack. Unfortunately, I hadn't taken the time to organise the garage, and Avril quickly became overwhelmed by the chaos. Tears started flowing as the stress of the situation mounted. Nela, who had come dressed for a lighter day helping Avril with clothes, ended up rolling up her sleeves and jumping in to help me haul greasy car engines and other car parts into my truck. She was a true trooper that day, and we couldn't have done it without her.

In the end, we got everything loaded onto the truck. While Nela and Avril finished cleaning the old house, we made our way to Hamilton, ready to begin this new chapter in our lives.

CHAPTER 37

Enjoying the Fruits of Our Labour

Settling into my house in Hamilton was a smooth and easy process. Having owned the property for many years and previously rented it out to students, I was already familiar with the neighbours, which made the transition even more seamless. After a couple of months of getting settled, I was eager to begin building my garage. I designed a plan for the structure and submitted it to the City of Hamilton for approval to obtain my building permit. Fortunately, the plan was approved, and I received the permit. However, before I could start construction, I needed to remove an 8x10-foot shed from the backyard. I carefully dismantled it and then reassembled it at one of my other properties.

My initial vision was to build a double-car garage with double doors, providing enough space to park two vehicles. Unfortunately, my backyard didn't have enough room to accommodate such a structure. I had to come up with a more creative solution. I devised an ingenious plan to build a garage that was one and a half times the size of a standard single-car garage, with a single entrance door. However, I wanted to be able to park two cars side by side in the garage. This is where I came up with the ingenious idea.

I built two wooden forms and placed them on the floor of the garage before the concrete was poured. The wooden forms were placed parallel to each other, with a distance between them matching the wheelbase of a large car. I had a truck deliver the concrete, and as the truck poured the concrete, my sons, Chris and Ian, helped me spread the mixture and complete the base of the garage floor. After the concrete had set, I removed the forms and lined the channels with steel tracks. I later built a ramp and bolted 32 heavy-duty caster wheels, each capable of supporting up to 10 tons.

The ramp was placed in the steel tracks, allowing it to roll smoothly from one side of the garage to the other. This clever system made it easy to drive one car onto the ramp and then push it with minimal effort to the opposite side of the garage. Once the first car was in place, I could simply drive the second car into the remaining space.

This entire project took me about a month to complete, with invaluable assistance from my ever-helpful partner, Avril. Thanks to my innovative design, I was finally able to comfortably park two cars in my new garage, making the space both functional and efficient.

As you may have guessed by now, I'm a huge fan of cars. Over the years, my garage and driveway have become home to some incredible vehicles. I parked Avril's sleek white Jaguar XF alongside my own blue Jaguar XF, while my trusty black Jaguar XJ8 sat nearby. My driveway was dominated by my old, rusty workhorse, the Dodge Ram 2500, which, despite its wear and tear, served me well for various tasks. I also had a 1929 Mercedes-Benz SSK replica parked in one of my student house garages.

I often refer to my Dodge Ram as my "workhorse" because that's exactly what it is. It was the vehicle I relied on for everything, from hauling materials from Home Depot to transporting shingles and student garbage to the dump. It might have been a rusty mess, but it got the job done. One day, while heading back from the dump, a woman followed me into a parking lot and said to me, "Sir, I was driving behind you, and your truck was flaking." We both had a good laugh about it. After many years of service, I decided it was time to get rid of my flaking truck. A week later, I sold my trusted Dodge Ram and drove off in a brand-new blue Ford F-150.

With the garage project complete and Hamilton life settling into a comfortable rhythm, I found myself turning attention to something a little more fun, my car. After years of loyalty to our Jaguars, I felt it was time to bring some of that Florida sunshine spirit home by getting a convertible car.

At my condo in Florida, I also owned a Jaguar XK8 convertible, and there's nothing quite like driving it with the top down on a sunny day. That got me thinking, since we have such beautiful summers in Canada. Avril had been driving a white Jaguar XF sedan, and I was driving a blue Jaguar XF sedan as well for quite some time. I felt it was time for a new adventure. I decided to trade in my blue Jaguar XF for a convertible sports car. We have been loyal Jaguar owners for many years, and I still wanted to stay within the Jaguar family.

We drove to the Jaguar dealership to test drive their new F-Type sports car. However, I didn't quite feel at home in it. The cockpit felt cramped, and I didn't think I had enough legroom to make it comfortable for long drives, so I quickly ruled it out.

Having previously owned several old Mercedes-Benz vehicles, I decided to visit the Mercedes dealership to explore my options. In 1976, while teaching in Jamaica, I bought an old 1964 Mercedes-Benz 280S, and I loved every minute of driving it. It was a symbol of status, and although maintenance was expensive due to its age, I didn't mind because I felt good driving it. Over the years, between 1981 and 1987, I owned several older Mercedes-Benz vehicles, including a Mercedes-Benz 280SEL, two 280SEs, and a 230S. While these cars were costly to maintain, I enjoyed the challenge of fixing them, and I had a deep appreciation for their engineering.

When I visited the Mercedes-Benz dealership and test drove the SL 550 hardtop convertible, I immediately fell in love with it. The drive was smooth, and the car felt like a perfect fit for me. It was everything I wanted in a convertible sports car, so I made the decision to purchase it right then and there.

With my new Mercedes convertible parked in the garage and our property management becoming more streamlined, Avril and I started thinking about how we wanted to spend our time moving forward. The answer was simple: we wanted to travel more, and with fewer properties to manage, we finally could.

Since our move to Hamilton, managing our properties has become significantly easier. Most of them were now located in Hamilton and St. Catharines, where I also maintained several properties, including my son Chris's; it was only about a 30-minute drive away. My son, Chris, had also invested in a couple of properties there.

Avril and I soon realised that we were dedicating too much of our time to managing these properties, and with age catching up to us, we knew it was time for a change. We decided to start liquidating some of our holdings, both in Canada and the United States, and to redirect our investments elsewhere. This decision opened new possibilities for us, giving us the freedom to travel more.

Our travels so far had been to Fiji, Australia, the Caribbean, South America, England, and the United States, and we were eager to explore more places. During one of our trips to England to visit Avril's family, we took the opportunity to board the Eurostar train that goes through the Chunnel to Paris, accompanied by the boys. We spent an entire week in Paris, which I thoroughly enjoyed, though I must admit, London remains my favourite city.

On another trip to England, we decided to make our Christmas getaway a bit more special by including a mini vacation beforehand. Morocco, with its warm climate and proximity to England, seemed like the perfect choice. Mark, Ian, and Alanna were already living in London, and Chris travelled with us, so all of us flew into Marrakech for a four-day vacation. Morocco, being one of the more secular Muslim countries, allowed us the freedom to explore. We wandered the Souks at leisure and even bought alcohol at designated supermarkets that sold it legally. However, Avril became quite concerned when Mark and Chris went to a nightclub, especially since Chris was already drunk by the time they left our hotel. Fortunately, they made friends at the club, drinking tea and chatting about football.

When travelling, it's almost a given that you'll be offered tours by official guides, usually at steep prices. However, I've always preferred seeking out locals who are willing to negotiate, often for half, or even less than half, the cost of those official tours. In Morocco, I found a local man in the Souks who had a cube van. He offered to take us to the Atlas Mountains for far less than what the official tour companies charged. Along the way, we stopped at various points of interest, including caves and a demonstration of ancient meal preparations. We even climbed the

Atlas Mountains, where we had a breathtaking view, with Tunisia visible on the other side. After our mountain trek, we enjoyed a lovely lunch with our driver before returning to Marrakech, where we paid him for his services. Everyone was content with the experience.

Our travels also took us to the south of France, to the beautiful city of Orange, where we rented a large villa complete with a swimming pool, along with the three boys and their girlfriends. Orange, a city rich in history and ancient treasures, was full of life, and during our stay, we took the opportunity to explore several charming southern French cities. The trip was a perfect mix of relaxation and adventure, and we made memories to last a lifetime.

These travels have enriched our lives in many ways, and they have given us the opportunity to create lasting memories with family, explore new cultures, and embrace the freedom that comes with slowing down.

CHAPTER 38

The World Was Ours to See

After returning from our trip to France, Avril and I were eager to explore more of Europe, so we decided to visit Italy. We flew into Rome, rented a car, and drove south to the city of Agropoli, which we used as a base for further adventures. From there, we explored other cities such as Sorrento, Pompeii, Naples, and the Amalfi Coast. We also took a ferry to the picturesque Isle of Capri.

It was the same year that the Manchester United football team was playing in the European Cup in Rome, and our son Chris, a die-hard Manchester United fan, flew to the city with a friend to watch the match. They travelled by bus or train (I'm not entirely sure which) and met us in Sorrento for a wonderful dinner in this charming town. When we asked where they were staying, they were a bit evasive, so we didn't press them. Later, we discovered that they had not booked any accommodation and had managed to persuade the owner of a rooftop bar where they had been drinking to let them sleep there overnight after the bar closed. The following day, they returned to Rome.

One of the most memorable experiences of the trip was visiting Pompeii. It's a truly fascinating city that should be on everyone's travel bucket list. The ancient city was tragically buried under a thick layer of volcanic ash and debris when Mount Vesuvius erupted in 79 AD. It remained preserved for centuries, only to be rediscovered in the 16th century. Walking through the ruins and seeing the remarkably well-preserved structures gives you a deep sense of history.

The Isle of Capri, on the other hand, didn't leave us a lasting impression. While the island boasts stunning high cliffs and hills, the beach was made up of large, uncomfortable pebbles. I couldn't help but feel sorry for the people lying on the stones, sunbathing; it must have been incredibly painful.

One of the highlights of our trip was driving along the Amalfi Coast. The road was winding, with sharp turns offering breathtaking views of the coastline, dotted with small towns nestled among the cliffs, and the sparkling blue Mediterranean Sea below. It was a beautiful drive that will stay in my memory forever.

We also made our way to Naples, where we drove up to the hilltop Castle Saint Elmo for a stunning panoramic view of the city and its busy port, where cruise ships dock. As we made our way to the viewpoint, I couldn't help but notice the damaged side mirrors on many parked cars. It's common in Italy to see vehicles, even expensive luxury ones, with dents and scratches that often go unrepaired. As a car enthusiast, I was horrified by the sight of it. Later, while looking for parking in the city, a taxi driver approached me and asked where I was from. When I told him, he laughed and said, "You must be crazy to drive here in Naples! Italians rarely do." I told him I had driven in Jamaica, which amused him even more.

Wanting to experience a little more of Rome, we checked out of our hotel in Agropoli a day early and drove back to the city, where we booked a new hotel. Driving in Italy was an experience; hundreds of motorbikes darted in and out of traffic, often ignoring the rules of the road. They create their own lanes, making it almost dizzying to watch. The roads are well-maintained, and due to the country's mountainous terrain, many tunnels cut through the mountains to avoid having to drive over them.

In Rome, we visited all the major tourist attractions, including the Colosseum, the Spanish Steps, and more. While walking around the Coliseum, I tripped over a loose cobblestone, so I decided to pick it up as a keepsake. I wrapped it in a magazine I had with me, and it now serves as a bookend in my home to keep my books in place.

We had an unforgettable time in Italy, soaking in the culture, history, and beauty of the country. Afterward, we flew back home to Canada, where we relished the warm summer weather.

After returning from Italy with memories of Pompeii, Sorrento, and the Amalfi Coast etched in our minds, we didn't have to wait long for another adventure. This time, it was a family celebration that would take us back to France. Mark and Gillian had chosen a stunning village in the south for their wedding.

During a family vacation in Orange, France, Mark and his girlfriend Gillian discovered their love for the region, particularly the south of France. They decided this was where they wanted to get married. They found a picturesque village called Aubeterre, nestled in the heart of the region.

In 2015, our entire family flew to London, where we met up with Avril's relatives. Together, we flew to Bordeaux, rented cars at the airport, and made our way to Aubeterre. The village was absolutely charming, with its town square perched atop a hill, offering sweeping views of the village below. The wedding was held in a most spectacular chateau that looked like a large castle, the name of it was Chateau le Mas de Montet. On the day of the wedding, Chris and I took a trip back to the airport to pick up Pat Ferretti, a long-time family friend. The wedding was followed by a stay at a stunning chateau with a swimming pool for four days, where the party continued, a truly unforgettable experience.

After the wedding, Mark and Gillian went to the French Alps for their honeymoon, while Avril, Chris, April, Ian, Alanna, and I headed to Barcelona, Spain. Once in Barcelona, we all split up to explore different parts of the city before reconvening in Lisbon, Portugal. From there, Ian and Alanna flew back to London, while Chris and April returned to Canada. It was a remarkable time of family bonding and adventure.

Avril and I went on a trip to Seville, Spain, after hearing glowing recommendations from several people who had visited. They were right; Seville is an incredibly beautiful city. As we wandered through its charming streets, I suddenly remembered the Seville oranges we have in Jamaica, which were brought to the island by the Spanish colonisers. These oranges are so common in Seville, and I noticed an abundance of orange trees throughout the city. Eager to share a piece of Jamaica with Avril, I picked one of the oranges and showed it to her, remarking that it was the same as the ones we have back home. Just then, a local man rushed up to us, shouting, "No eat, no eat, no good!" He clearly didn't know that in Jamaica, we don't eat these oranges either; they are primarily used to make marmalade.

While in Seville, we were also fortunate to reconnect with a long-lost relative. My sister Sherron had discovered our cousin on Facebook, my mother's brother, Arthur Hoilet, who had migrated to England in the 1950s as part of the Windrush generation. Arthur had settled in England, started a family, and one of his daughters, Karlene (Kari) Hoilet had later moved to Spain, where she bought an olive and fig farm. She kindly drove to Seville, picked us up, and took us to her farm, located deep in the heart of Spain in a small town called Los Santos De Maimona, where the temperature was over 100 degrees Fahrenheit. We spent about a week there, enjoying the peaceful countryside and catching up on the stories of our uncle and his other children. In between sharing family memories, we also explored the area and did a few touristy things, which made for an unforgettable experience.

When it was time to leave, our cousin drove us to the bus stop, where we caught a bus to Lisbon, from which we flew back to Canada, feeling grateful for the wonderful experiences we had in Spain.

Our time in Spain after the wedding, from Seville to Lisbon, felt like a beautiful extension of the celebration. When we returned home, refreshed and reflective, Avril began seriously considering retirement. With both of us free from work obligations, we felt it was time to plan our next big journey, and this one would take us deep into the heart of Europe.

After I retired from my position at TD Canada Trust, Avril continued working as a realtor for a while. However, her heart wasn't fully in it. We were travelling frequently, enjoying time at our condo in Florida, which led Avril to temporarily put her real estate licence on hold. This decision to step back from her career made it easier for us to travel freely and pursue whatever adventures we wanted without any constraints.

During my time as an IT consultant, I spent a considerable amount of time on the golf course with my dear friend Ron

Austriaco, who has since passed away, and Joan Hart, with whom I'm still in touch. Avril, too, had taken up golf when she entered the real estate world. She took lessons and began playing regularly with her friend Ellen Peddle. Now that we were both retired, we enjoyed spending more time together on the golf course.

With Avril's retirement, we found ourselves even more eager to explore new destinations. There was nothing holding us back. Our sons, Ian and Chris, were more than capable of handling any emergencies that might arise with the student houses while we were away, and I had made arrangements with repairmen in Florida to handle any urgent repairs, especially for things like the air conditioning and refrigerators.

By February or May of 2017, Avril and I began discussing our next big adventure. We pulled up a map of Europe on the computer and started brainstorming destinations that interested us. Amsterdam, Netherlands, had long been on my bucket list, so I suggested to Avril that while we were exploring the eastern part of Europe, we could extend our trip to include Belgium, Switzerland, Austria, the Czech Republic, Germany, and England. We agreed on this exciting itinerary, and it was time to plan the details.

We started by researching the most popular cities in each country to visit, deciding how many days we would spend in each location. Amsterdam was already on our list for the Netherlands, while Bruges was our choice for Belgium. Geneva stood out for Switzerland, Vienna for Austria, Prague for the Czech Republic, Berlin for Germany, and finally, we would visit our son and his family in London. Our European journey was taking shape!

Our journey spanned six weeks, filled with train and plane rides, and stays at various hotels and Airbnbs. We meticulously planned our trip in advance, ensuring we had all our bookings for hotels, Airbnbs, train tickets, and plane tickets in hand before embarking on our adventure.

CHAPTER 39

Europe in Full Bloom: From Windmills to the Berlin Wall

Our first destination was Amsterdam, where we flew into Schiphol Airport. We stayed at a hotel conveniently located near the airport, with easy access to the city centre via a short bus ride. We spent four enjoyable days exploring Amsterdam, taking a memorable trip to a windmill farm, and hopping on local buses to see all that the city had to offer. One of the more daring moments of our trip was when Avril challenged me to ask one of the women in the Red-Light District's windows about her rates. I did and learned that the price was 50 euros. The air in the city was thick with the unmistakable scent of marijuana, which seemed to hang over the streets. Dining out in Amsterdam was surprisingly more affordable than in Canada, which was a pleasant surprise.

Although Dutch is the primary language spoken in Amsterdam, I was impressed by how nearly 90% of the locals were fluent in English, making communication effortless. Our time in

Amsterdam was filled with great experiences, but it was soon time to head to our next destination: Bruges, Belgium.

We arrived in Bruges and checked into the hotel we had booked ahead of time. The hotel was charming, albeit somewhat old-fashioned and different from the more modern hotels we had previously stayed in across Europe. Our stay was enjoyable, though the experience was occasionally interrupted by sounds from the adjacent room, as the walls were far from soundproof, and we could hear some rather explicit sexual noises coming from next door. Bruges itself was a picturesque city, with canals weaving through its streets. We took a delightful boat cruise that allowed us to see the city from a unique perspective.

We also visited a local brewery that boasted an impressive selection of 500 different beers. We sampled a few and even purchased two half-litre bottles, each with our names and pictures emblazoned on the labels as souvenirs. I was surprised to find so many visitors from the UK in Bruges. A local told us that it's a popular spot for Brits due to its proximity to England, something I confirmed later by checking the map.

As someone with more conservative tastes in food, I ventured outside my comfort zone and tried the Belgian national dish, Moules-Frites. It wasn't bad, but I can't say I'd order it again. The typical dining hour for Belgians is between 7 p.m. and 8 p.m., but I found it fascinating that when I was out at 11 p.m., the sun was still shining brightly, and the restaurants were still buzzing with activity, filled with people enjoying their meals well into the late hours of the evening.

Geneva, Switzerland, is an exquisitely beautiful city that left a lasting impression on us during our visit. We had the pleasure of staying at a delightful hotel nestled in the very heart of the city, just a short walk from the iconic Lake Geneva. The lake itself is absolutely breathtaking, with its pristine, crystal-clear waters that shimmer in the sunlight. It's no surprise that both locals and tourists flock to this stunning location, especially for leisurely beach outings. We were fortunate enough to take a dip in the refreshing waters, which was a highlight of our trip and an experience we will never forget.

From the city, the view of the Monts de Genève Mountains standing majestically in the background is simply awe-inspiring. At times, the peaks looked like a snow-capped mountain, further enhancing the natural beauty of the scene. Later, I learned that at elevations above 10,000 feet, the temperature drops below freezing, causing moisture to accumulate on the summit and transform into snow and ice. This process creates the mesmerizing snow-capped look we were so fortunate to witness during our stay.

As a truly global hub, Geneva is home to a wide array of international organisations and major financial institutions. During one of our meals at a cosy local restaurant, we had the unique opportunity to meet two Nigerian diplomats who were in the city for an international conference. Their presence added an intriguing cultural and political dimension to our time in Geneva, making our experience even more enriching.

However, as we discovered firsthand, Geneva is notorious for its high cost of living. The city's expensive housing market has made it increasingly unaffordable for many residents, and some locals shared with us that it can be a significant financial burden. In fact, many people choose to purchase homes in nearby French towns and commute to Geneva for work, as it offers a more financially viable alternative to living within the city itself. This phenomenon is a testament to the city's high living expenses, despite the many advantages it offers as a cosmopolitan and vibrant destination.

Vienna, Austria, is a stunning city renowned for its picturesque parks, rolling hills, and impressive architectural landmarks. During our stay, we booked an Airbnb that was conveniently located near the subway, making it just a 15-minute ride to the heart of the city. To explore Vienna's most famous tourist attractions, we opted for a hop-on-hop-off bus tour, which allowed us to see the city at our own pace.

I had always assumed that Adolf Hitler was born in Germany, but I was surprised to learn during the tour that he was actually born in Austria. As we travelled through Vienna, the tour guide pointed out the men's dormitory located at Meldemannstraße 27 in the district of Brigittenau, where Hitler lived from 1910 to 1913. This public dormitory for men played a significant role in his early years.

Vienna is famously known as the "City of Music," and we got to experience this firsthand as we listened to various bands perform in the city's beautiful parks. One of the highlights of our trip was a scenic boat cruise along the Danube River, which winds through the centre of the city, offering breathtaking views of Vienna's skyline and surrounding landmarks.

We took a flight from Vienna to Prague, and it was a stunning journey with breathtaking views of the snow-capped mountains stretching across the horizon. Upon arrival, we were immediately taken in by the charm of Prague, a city renowned for its magnificent architecture, which shares similarities with many other grand European cities. Though the Czech Republic uses its own currency, the Czech Crown, the euro is also widely accepted. Our stay in Prague was made even more memorable by a lovely Airbnb apartment that offered panoramic views of the city, including the train station where we first arrived.

One of the highlights of our trip was visiting Prague Castle to witness the Changing of the Guards, an impressive ceremony reminiscent of the one at Buckingham Palace in London. The soldiers, adorned in striking sky-blue uniforms, stood proudly as a military band played their trumpets, creating an unforgettable spectacle.

The Vltava River, which runs through the heart of Prague, has played a vital role in the city's history for centuries, with the city gradually developing around its banks. We embarked on a scenic boat cruise along the river, passing under the iconic Charles Bridge, which dates back to 1870. There is a popular local legend that eggs were used in the construction of the bridge, a curious tidbit shared by our tour guide. Whether this story is true or not, it certainly added an interesting layer to the historical narrative.

In an unexpected turn of events, we encountered Jehovah's Witnesses not at the door of a house, but in a restaurant in Prague. It turns out there was a Jehovah's Witnesses conference in the city, and they seemed eager to strike up a conversation with us. Rather than engage in religious discussions, Avril and I skilfully redirected the conversation, asking them about their hometowns, their experiences in Prague, and their families.

Our four days in Prague passed by in a blur, just as quickly as in the previous cities we had explored. We packed our suitcases, bidding farewell to the adorable cat that had kept us company during our stay. The Airbnb host had asked if we were comfortable with the cat staying there, and of course, we did not mind at all, as we have two cats of our own back home.

As we made our way downhill toward the train station, rolling our suitcases behind us, we were met with a commotion. The station was cordoned off, and there was a significant presence of military and police personnel. We soon learned that there had been a bomb threat at the station, just a week after the devastating terrorist bombing in Paris. The station was in complete chaos as thousands of travellers were stranded, unable to board or depart on any train.

The authorities swiftly redirected the crowds to a nearby park, where they tried to organise buses to other stations, but the situation was one of complete confusion. For us, the urgency of the situation was growing as we needed to catch a train to another city in the Czech Republic, where we were supposed to transfer to a train bound for Berlin, Germany. The transportation system was struggling to accommodate the masses, and there simply were not enough buses.

Determined to sort things out on our own, Avril and I bought a map of Prague that included bus and train routes. Armed with the map, we managed to catch a local bus that took us to a smaller train station, where we were able to board the train we had originally booked to Berlin. The journey to Berlin was smooth and picturesque, offering views of rolling mountains, winding rivers, lush parks, and charming farms. As the train passed through various towns, we were captivated by the diversity of houses and the beauty of the landscapes, making it a perfect conclusion to our adventure.

After an incredibly busy day, we finally arrived in Berlin, Germany. We had already booked our hotel, which was conveniently located near the train station. Once we grabbed our suitcases, we took a short walk to the hotel and checked in. Situated right in the heart of Berlin, the hotel's location allowed us to easily explore the city on foot, with many of the main tourist attractions just a short stroll away.

As we walked around, one thing that stood out to me was the extensive construction taking place all over the city. There were cranes everywhere, and it was clear that Berlin was in the midst of a transformation. The city had a vibrant, cosmopolitan feel, like other major European cities such as Amsterdam and Geneva. However, it had a distinct energy that set it apart from places like Vienna and Prague. I was particularly struck by how common it was to see locals sitting outside, enjoying themselves in the most unexpected spots, whether in a parking lot or a park, often with a drink in their hands. Wine and beer flowed freely in public spaces, adding to the relaxed and open atmosphere.

During our stay, we took part in a variety of tours, both bus and walking. The city's history is truly captivating, not only because of the atrocities that occurred there but also because of the extraordinary ways in which some of these events unfolded. Berlin's complex past, particularly its division during the Cold War, has been the subject of countless books. One of the most striking aspects of our tour was learning about the sudden and dramatic division of Germany. The tour guide explained how, overnight, German soldiers erected 30 miles of barbed wire along the border between East and West Berlin, with checkpoints running through cemeteries, streets, and even subway stations. The next day, families who had once lived together found themselves separated, with some members now living as East Germans and others as West Germans.

We thoroughly enjoyed our time in Berlin, hopping on various tour buses to explore the city and sampling the local cuisine at numerous restaurants. German beers and wines were a delightful part of the experience, and we relished the opportunity to soak in both the history and the vibrant culture of the city.

After a wonderful stay in Berlin, we flew to London, England, where we were excited to reunite with our son Mark and his family. We spent the next couple of weeks in England, splitting our time between Mark, Gillian, and our lovely granddaughters, Freya and Lily, as well as Avril's family in East Anglia, Norfolk. It was a wonderful family gathering, and we cherished every moment spent with loved ones.

CHAPTER 40

<hr>

Legacy, Reflections, and the Life We Built

Mark completed a business degree at Sir Wilfrid Laurier University in Waterloo. He is married to Gillian Davis, and they have two girls, Freya and Lily. He is a Quantitative Surveyor in senior management at an international engineering consulting company.

Chris pursued his accounting degree at Brock University, but unlike his brothers, who were more interested in travelling the world, he focused on real estate investment. After completing his studies, he initially worked at Loblaw but soon found the role lacking in challenge. Seeking more fulfilling work, Chris transitioned to a position as a forensic accountant specialising in business interruptions at an insurance company. However, he did not enjoy the office environment and opted to work from his home office, a setup he has maintained for over a decade. Following in my footsteps, Chris became a successful real estate investor. He owned several student rental properties near Brock University in St. Catharines, Canada, and has expanded his portfolio with several properties in Florida. Chris and his wife, April Greacen, are proud parents to four children: Ruby, Lyla, Finley, and Theo.

Ian completed his business degree at McMaster University in Hamilton, Canada. After graduating, he followed in the footsteps of his older brother, Mark, and travelled to London, England, with his girlfriend, Alanna Boyle. Ian secured a job at the BBC in the procurement department, which was a role he was familiar with from his internship at Dofasco, a steel company based in Hamilton.

Ian worked at the BBC for several years. During that time, he expressed interest in transitioning to the production side of the business. His manager, recognising his potential, allowed him to shadow production workers on Fridays. This led to Ian being hired in the production department, where he contributed to shoots for commercials and gained invaluable hands-on experience.

After six years in England, Ian and Alanna decided they were ready to return to Canada and settle down. However, before heading home, they made one final stop in Australia. They flew to Sydney, where Ian secured a position at Fox Television, thanks to a colleague he had worked with at the BBC. This move allowed them to explore Australia, and it proved to be a great opportunity for them both.

On their way home from Australia, they took a detour and decided to travel through Asia. They visited several countries, including China, South Korea, Vietnam, Japan, Singapore, and more. By the end of their seven years abroad, Ian and Alanna had visited 61 countries across all seven continents.

Upon returning to Canada, Ian leveraged his extensive international experience to land a job at TSN, a sports television station in Toronto. His global perspective and expertise led him to a senior management role at the network. Now that they had settled back in Canada, Ian and Alanna decided to tie the knot. They planned a destination wedding at the Bahia Principe resort in Runaway Bay, Jamaica, with guests attending from all over the world, including England, the United States, Alaska, Australia, New Zealand, Jamaica, and Canada. These were friends he had made on their travelling excursions.

The wedding itself was a stunning outdoor affair held on a beautiful white sand beach, with the turquoise Caribbean Sea providing a breathtaking backdrop. Ian and Alanna are now proud parents of two children, Callum and Brooke.

Reflecting on the lives and accomplishments of my three sons fills me with immense pride. But as a Black father in Canada, witnessing their success has also made me think more deeply about the broader realities we have had to navigate as a family, particularly the subtle and not-so-subtle ways racism still exists in this country we call home.

Canada is my adopted home, and I am incredibly grateful for it. I love this country and would not want to live anywhere else, except my country of birth, Jamaica. However, I feel compelled to address an important issue in this book that cannot be overlooked: systemic racism. As a Black person living in Canada, I have personally encountered various forms of systemic racism. While some individuals, particularly among the white community, might deny the existence of systemic racism here, they cannot truly understand the lived experiences of Black people unless they have walked in our shoes.

Crimes are committed by individuals of all races, including Black, brown, and white people. However, even though only a very small fraction of the Black population is involved in criminal activity, the actions of that tiny minority often lead to the stigmatisation of all Black individuals. The vast majority of Black people are law-abiding citizens, just like any other race. As part of that vast majority, we too want those individuals who commit crimes to face justice, just like people of any other race. I have many white friends, and I do not judge them based on the unlawful actions of others in their community. I judge them based on their character, and I believe that is how we should treat everyone, regardless of their race.

Cultural differences are a significant factor in the misunderstandings that can arise between people of different backgrounds. However, by trying to understand one another's culture, we can bridge the gap and foster better relationships. The younger generations today have the benefit of growing up in a more integrated society, where cultural diversity is more visible in schools, sports, and community organisations. As someone who has coached culturally diverse baseball teams for 16 years, I have witnessed firsthand how these children grow into adulthood with lasting friendships across cultural lines.

Despite living in Canada and enjoying financial success, I have still experienced instances of systemic racism. There have been times when I have been pulled over by the police while driving my Jaguar. On two separate occasions, officers stopped me and asked, "Who owns this car?" On one of these occasions, when I inquired about the reason for the stop, one officer explained that they had suspected the car might be stolen.

I have also experienced subtle forms of racism in other situations. For example, I owned a large 4,000-square-foot home by a golf course, with two Jaguars parked in the driveway. A cable repairman, who was at my home to do some work, had to call his office for permission to do something outside of his work order.

I overheard him telling the person on the phone that the home-owner was not at the house. When I approached him, I said, "You may not think I look like the homeowner, but I am the owner." He was visibly embarrassed and quickly apologised.

Another experience took place when my wife Avril and I returned from our four-month winter stay at our condo in Florida. A new neighbour had moved across the street during our absence and had met Avril, who is white, but had not yet met me. On a sunny day, I was washing my cars, two Jaguars, a Mercedes-Benz SL 550, and my Ford F150 pickup truck, in the driveway. The new neighbour came over and asked if I was a car washer and if I could wash his car as well. I explained to him that all the cars were mine and invited him to look at my 1929 Mercedes-Benz SSK, which was parked in the garage. His surprise was evident, and I could see that his assumptions had been shattered.

These experiences, while frustrating, are just a few examples of the subtle yet pervasive forms of systemic racism that exist in Canada. It is important to recognise and address these issues, but it is equally important to remember that the vast majority of individuals, regardless of race, are good, law-abiding citizens who deserve to be judged based on their actions and character, not stereotyped.

While these experiences have been frustrating at times, they have not defined our lives, far from it. Today, Avril and I continue to live with purpose, surrounded by the family we raised and the joy we worked so hard to create. Our days now look a little different, but they are rich in love, laughter, and a deep appreciation for the journey we have walked.

At this stage in our lives, we cherish spending time with our grandchildren. It is always a joy to visit them and attend their sports events. When we are back in Canada, we dedicate our weekends to the six grandchildren who live nearby. It is a time we deeply value and look forward to.

Every year, sometimes twice per year, we make it a priority to travel to England to visit our granddaughters there. This yearly trip has become a tradition, and it is something we truly look forward to.

During the colder months, we escape to Florida, where we not only enjoy the warm weather but also indulge in the pleasures of cruising to explore new destinations. Florida has become our second home, and while we are there, we often travel to other countries, discovering new cultures and experiences along the way. We also take frequent trips to Jamaica while we are in Florida.

Our three sons and their families join us in Florida at various points during the winter months, creating cherished moments together. Their visits are something we eagerly anticipate, as they allow us to spend even more quality time with them and our grandkids, whom we adore and miss when we are in Florida.

In addition to family time, we have a wonderful group of friends who also own condos in Fort Lauderdale. Jim and Joan Hart, along with Don and Nela Clark, are fellow Canadians, and we enjoy socialising with them. We spend countless hours playing golf, relaxing on the beach, dining out, or simply unwinding by the pool with a refreshing adult beverage in hand. These are the moments that make life so enjoyable.

I truly hope you have enjoyed reading my story. For many Jamaicans, especially those who grew up in the countryside, I believe parts of my journey will strike a familiar chord. Whether it is the struggles, the sacrifices, or the small joys of a simple life, I know my roots are shared by countless others.

Today, I consider myself incredibly blessed to live the life I do. But make no mistake, while we enjoy the fruits of our labour, we never take any of it for granted. Every step of the way has been grounded in perseverance, faith, and hard work. My wife, Avril, and I often reflect on how far we have come, always with a sense of humility and gratitude for the opportunities we have been given and the ones we created for ourselves.

I sometimes tell Avril that if I had the chance to live my life all over again, I would not change much. Even though I started with very little in Jamaica, those early years gave me more than material wealth ever could. The discipline, resilience, and sense of purpose I developed back then became the foundation for everything I have accomplished since. Those humble beginnings were not a disadvantage; they were a blessing in disguise.

Thank you for taking this journey with me.

Wedding

Pictures

Our wedding day

Avril and her dad

Graduation day with Avril

Vic my bestman

Chris & his wife April

Mark & Gill's wedding

Ian and Alanna's wedding in Jamaica

Before grand children

Picture from my wedding

Ian & Alanna's wedding

Ian's wedding party
at Tatchil, Ocho Rios,
Jamaica

Hanging out in Mile
End

Family

Pictures

Brooke chilling on the rock

Callum chilling

Lily chilling

Freya chilling

Lyla in Florida

These cuties are our 8 grandchildren

Ruby my eldest granddaughter

Finley & Theo, 2-peas in a pod.

Me at Mico University College

My cousin Pastor Ray

My grandfather Daddy

Avril, my beautiful wife

Camping with my 3 boys

Avril 23 year old girl I met in Spanish Town Jamaica

Inside the gate of our house, we called the Ranch in Spanish Town

Avril, my father and grandchildren

My mother, brothers and sisters

My biological father Vincent Davis

Me, with my 2 half brothers and sister and her daughter

Avril in the Spitfire, her dad flew

Our young family

242

Nathan my cousin, we hangout together as boys

Mammy, my grandmother right & her sister aunt Flarey

My mother and sister aunt Pearl

Avril's parents Maurice & Mary

Maurice Avril's dad, who flew Spitfire and Mustang in WW II

Vic, Rozzie, Avril, and I

Friend

♡

Pictures

My friend Eddie Cousins at his mining company

Malcolm and I hanging out at Niagara Falls

Hanging with friends Burrell, me, Prince & Clyde

1977 Rick's Cafe, Negril Jamaica with Sue and friends

Dunns River Falls with Prince & Malcolm

St. Catherine High School Spanish Town

A tradition to bury Teaching Practice at Mico

Florida group, me, Avril, Nela, Don, Jean & Jim

Avril and her friend Sue

Ahn Phan My protege

Baseball

Pictures

BRAMPTON
B
MINOR BASEBALL
1992

Chris baseball team

BRAMPTON
B
MINOR BASEBALL
1997

Ian's Baseball team

Mark at his high school football game

Me the baseball coach

250

Mark's baseball team

BRAMPTON MINOR BASEBALL
1990

M. Jones Photo
454-8952

Baseball coaches for
Chris Rep team, Chuck,
me & Monty

Places Of

Interest

The Family house in Jamaica)

Mass Butt shop

The shop my mother
sent me to when I was
a little boy

The river I crossed to
school & where my
mother washed our
clothes

Newstead All Age school

Mico University Colege
Kingston Jamaica

My nostalgic visit to
Concordia University

We were the Janitor of
this building

Our house before we downsized

The house we downsized to in Hamilton, Ontario

The garage I built at my house in Hamilton

One of my student houses

One of the buildings in which I owned condos

Car

Pictures

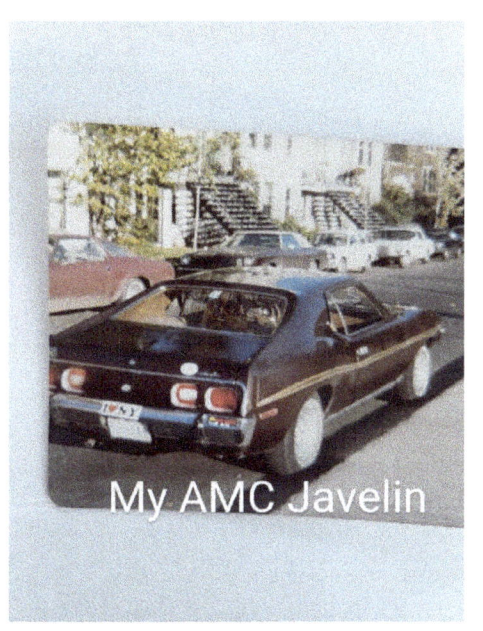

My AMC Javelin

My old 1964 Mercedes Benz 280 S

Posing on My Anglia

Avril's Jaguar F-Pace

One of my Mercedes Benz 280 SE

Building my 1929 Mercedes Benz SSK replica

Working on the Beetle for sale

The Beetle I paid $75 for and sold for $1,900

My blue Jaguar XF

Removing a Jaguar
engine to do a rebuild

My 1998 Jaguar XJ8 VDP

My 1994 Jaguar XJ8 VDP

My 1929 Mercedes

My Mercedes Benz SL
550 & Jaguar
XK8

Avril's S-Type Jaguar

Avril's Jaguar XF

www.ingramcontent.com/pod-product-compliance
Lightning Source LLC
Chambersburg PA
CBHW051137120626
46547CB00012B/839